Horizon of Secondary Education in Arunachal Pradesh

Problems and Prospects

Boa Reena Tok

Published by

ATLANTIC

PUBLISHERS & DISTRIBUTORS (P) LTD

7/22, Ansari Road, Darya Ganj, New Delhi-110002
Phones : +91-11-40775252, 40775214, 23273880, 23275880
Fax: +91-11-23285873
Web: www.atlanticbooks.com
E-mail: orders@atlanticbooks.com

Disclaimer

- The author and the publisher have taken every effort to the maximum of their skill, expertise and knowledge to provide correct material in the book. Even then if some mistakes persist in the content of the book, the publisher does not take responsibility for the same. The publisher shall have no liability to any person or entity with respect to any loss or damage caused, or alleged to have been caused directly or indirectly, by the information contained in this book.
- The author has fully tried to follow the copyright law. However, if any work is found to be similar, it is unintentional and the same should not be used as defamatory or to file legal suit against the author.
- If the readers find any mistakes, we shall be grateful to them for pointing out those to us so that these can be corrected in the next edition.
- All disputes are subject to the jurisdiction of Delhi courts only.

Printed & bound in India by Atlantic Print Services

Preface

The present book is based on the outcome of a major research project financed by Indian Council of Social Science Research (ICSSR) on the development, administrative structure, learning outcomes, problems, and the existing facilities available for the secondary school education in Arunachal Pradesh. It investigates and analyses the present scenario of secondary education in Arunachal Pradesh taking ground label data from the twenty districts of the state.

The book has five chapters discussing the scenario of secondary education in Arunachal Pradesh. The first chapter gives the introduction of secondary education in India in general and in Arunachal Pradesh in particular. It includes topics such as importance of secondary education, recommendations of commissions on secondary education, educational scenario in Arunachal Pradesh, an overview of the related literature, and achievements under *samagra shiksha* in Arunachal Pradesh. The next chapter makes a review of related literature on development and problems in the field of secondary education. The third chapter studies the methodology of the study including topics such as research design and method adopted in the present study, selection of the districts for the study, description of the population of the study, sample and sampling procedure, research tools used, procedure for data collection, data treatment and statistical techniques employed. The next chapter analyses and interprets the whole study using the data obtained from the field. The final chapter of the book includes the main findings and educational implications of the study.

The book will be beneficial to the policy makers, educationist, bureaucrats, research scholars, and those interested in the development of the education.

Boa Reena Tok

Contents

List of Tables

List of Figures

List of Map

1
Introduction

The Context

The level of growth and development of a nation can be gauged by examining the moral, intellectual, and professional status of its younger generation. The future of a country depends on its youths whose overall development depends on the system of education prevalent in that country. In turn, the competence of such a system depends on all the institutions that form the system. Therefore, it is essential to look at problems that hinder the efficiency of these institutions in various areas and to varying extents. Every educational institution has to be administered on systematic lines so as to yield good results. In principle, many policies have been implemented by the Government for the development of secondary education but in term of practical application, the various tenets associated with it have been neglected. Research evidences show that the secondary education is the fastest growing sector in most of the countries, further emphasizing the need of universalisation of it. Though secondary education forms an integral part in the development of the entire education system, very few studies have examined the related issues and problems associated with it in different regions of our country. In the context of our deteriorating education system, there exists a pressing need to enlighten the government and non-government organisations about the crucial problems of schools, so that they can take proper steps to improve the management and administration of the schools.

Secondary education is a crucial junction in the educational ladder as it provides two options for the students—(i) it prepares the students for higher studies, and (ii) it gives the opportunity to enter the job market to those students who are not able to continue their studies. The way education is increasingly linked to knowledge, skills, and employment at each stage has its relevance in the development of human capital. Of late, state policies have rightly prioritized elementary education as a thrust area and have demarcated higher education for research and development. But the secondary education, which is the main link between elementary and higher education, has remained neglected not only at policy level but also in research and analysis. According to the Secondary Education Commission (1952–53), "The secondary education must make itself responsible for equipping its students adequately with civic as well as vocational efficiency—and the qualities of character that go with it—so that they may be able to play their part worthy and competently in the improvement of national life". Thus, the quality of secondary education determines the development and quality of higher education. Therefore, a prerequisite for a productive education system is to have a better and improved secondary education with skill development and quality education.

Since independence there has been considerable expansion of secondary education in India. Following the Mudaliar Commission Report (1952–53), efforts have been made to revamp the secondary school system though without much success. The National Education Commission (1964–66), popularly known as Kothari Commission, made several recommendations to improve the quality, content, and methodology of teaching in secondary schools. The National Policy on Education (1968) pleaded for extended secondary education facilities to areas and classes of population which had been denied these in the past. The policy attempted to relate education to work and employment by introducing Socially Useful Productive Work (SUPW) and emphasized vocational education and technical education as components of secondary education. However, it still remains an unfulfilled goal due to non-functional vocational courses, practically lacking untrained teachers, absence of proper linkages with the related industries, and acceptance of vocational stream as inferior by both students and parents in our society. In this perspective secondary education is considered as midway for higher learning and the importance of it has been realized in education which will be discussed in the following section.

Importance of Secondary Education

Education is an important part of a person's life, which enables her/him to gain the skills that are needed to face the challenges of life. Every person should get the opportunity of gaining the right education as much as s/he wants. As part of the process of gaining the right education, it is necessary for a person to have secondary education, which is one of the key aspects of mainstream education after which the higher education follows.

According to the West Bengal Secondary Education Act, 1950, (passed by the West Bengal Legislature to provide for the regulation, control, and development of secondary education in West Bengal), "secondary education means education suitable to the requirements of all pupils who have completed primary education and includes general, technical, industrial, agricultural, and commercial education". Hence, secondary education is the final stage of school education that is imparted during adolescence. This stage is characterised by transition from a comprehensive elementary education to optional and selective form of training. In this stage, a child develops in-depth knowledge on specialized subjects. It is the extension of elementary education and forms the basis for higher education. It is assumed that secondary education was initially conceived as a preparatory course for students joining the higher studies in college. But, now it is concerned with all round personality development of the students. Therefore, secondary education must provide necessary background for the overall well-being of the students. According to International Commission on Education for Twenty-First Century, human beings live in four planes—physical, intellectual, mental, and spiritual. To support education at these four planes, the Commission identified four pillars of learning—learning to know, learning to do, learning to live together, and learning to be. The stage of secondary and higher secondary educations is a terminal stage for some and transition stage for others. In both the situations, the stage turns out to be the most important for the future of an individual. Thus, it is vital for every individual student to have secondary education, because it serves a link between elementary and higher education stages. It is the stage where a student acquires and enhances much vital knowledge that helps a growing mind to think, analyse, and study the world around.

Mission Objectives of Secondary Education

The vision for secondary education is to make good quality education available, accessible, and affordable to all young persons in the age group of 14–18 years. With this vision in mind, the following are to be achieved:

- To provide a secondary school within a reasonable distance of any habitation—within 5 kilometres for a secondary school and 7–10 kilometres for a higher secondary school.
- To ensure universal access of secondary education along with universal retention.
- To provide access to secondary education with special reference to economically weaker section of the society, the girls, children with special needs, and other marginalized categories like SC, ST, OBC, and EBM (Educationally Backward Minorities).

Recommendations of Commissions on Secondary Education

Secondary education cannot be treated only as a production function of the economy, neither it can be justified only on the ground that it contributes to human capital formation and provides an opportunity to large majority of school students to enter the work force. Conceptually, it should be inclusively justified on the ground that every child has right to exercise her/his potential and achieve excellence; education has the potentiality and state has the responsibility to facilitate such environment where a child can unfold her/his potential and achieve the excellence hidden in her/him. As per Central Advisory Board of Education (CABE) Report (2005), secondary education spreads over the ages of 15 and 16, and then to 17 and 18 in the senior secondary grades. These are the years of adolescence, and late adolescence; indeed, the most crucial transition periods of life. Thus, secondary education essentially has to be the education of adolescence. This is an appropriate stage which provides students a sense of national perspective to understand their constitutional duties and rights as citizens. In this stage they properly understand work ethos, human values, and culture. It means that the secondary and higher secondary levels are major instruments of social change and transformation.

Importance of secondary education led to appointment of several committees and commissions from time again to improve its quality by inspecting the lacuna prevailing in the secondary education system in the country. However, previous commissions and committees such as Indian Education Commission (1882) (also known as Hunter Commission), Saddler University Commission (1917–19), and University Education Commission (1948–49) (also known as Radhakrishnan Commission) all dealt with only certain aspects of the secondary education. They did not deal directly with the problems of secondary education. After independence, democratic government, educational philosophers, and social reformers of India felt the necessity of formulating new aims of education based on Indian culture and democratic principles. The then Prime Minister of India Pt. Jawaharlal Nehru remarked, "Great changes have taken place in the country and the educational system must also be in keeping with them. The entire basis of education must be revolutionized". It led to the formation of Secondary Education Commission (1952–53) under the chairmanship of Dr. A. Lakshmanswami Mudaliar to study comprehensively and specifically the prevalent condition of secondary education in India. Accordingly, the Commission analysed every aspects of secondary education in India in detail and after that formulated the following four aims of secondary education:

1. To produce ideal citizens,
2. To develop capacity for earning money,

3. To improve the quality of leadership, and
4. To develop human virtues.

The National Education Commission (1964–66), popularly known as Kothari Commission, was an ad hoc commission set up by the Government of India on 14th July, 1964, under the chairmanship of Dr. D.S. Kothari to examine all aspects of the education sector in India, to evolve a general pattern of education, and to advise guidelines and policies for the development of education at all stages and in all aspects. The main recommendations of the commission were:

1. Education should be developed so as to increase productivity, achieve social and national integration, accelerate the process of modernization, and cultivate social, moral, and spiritual values.
2. Science education should become an integral part of school education.
3. Social and national service should be an integral part of education at all stages.
4. Work experience should be introduced as an integral part of all education—general or vocational.
5. Stress should be given on vocational education.
6. Regional languages should be the medium of education at all stages of education.
7. Establishment of multi-purpose school.
8. Establishment of Central Board of Secondary Education and text book committee.

National Education Policy (NPE-1968)—Based on the report and recommendations of Kothari Commission (1964–66), Government of India formed a parliamentary committee on 4th April, 1967, and announced the first National Policy on Education in 1968, which called for a 'radical restructuring' and proposed equal educational opportunities in order to achieve national integration and greater cultural and economic development. The basic features of this policy relating to secondary education were:

1. Organization of education is a joint responsibility of the central and state governments.
2. Six percent of the central budget will be spent on education.
3. 10+2+3 pattern of education will be implemented in the whole country.
4. Secondary education will be expanded and upgraded.
5. "Three language formula" will be implemented at secondary level and that is Hindi, English, and regional language.
6. Work experience and national service will be made compulsory in the first ten years of education.
7. Economic aid will be given to the poor children studying in schools.
8. Reform examination system at all levels of education.
9. Organization of co-curricular activities.
10. Special management will be made for agricultural, vocational, technical, and engineering education.
11. Text books of high standard will be prepared for all levels of education.

Ishwarbhai Patel Committee (1977) was appointed to review the objectives and curriculum of ten year school system, in which the committee recommended the term "Socially Useful Productive Work (SUPW)" to "Work Experience (WE)" and recommended that SUPW to be an integral part of curriculum at all stages of school education. The committee formulated the following objectives of secondary education:

1. Acquisition of skills and habits of self learning.
2. Acquisition of a broad-based general education consisting of science, mathematics, social science, languages, and socially useful productive work.
3. Acquisition of habits of helpful living and participation in games, sports, and athletics for the maintenance of physical fitness.

4. Developing aesthetic appreciation and creativity through participation in artistic activities.
5. Exploring the world of work and understanding the realities of life in order to prepare for a confident entry into the world outside the school.
6. Participation in and promotion of social activities in school and community in such a way as to imbibe democratic values and to the work towards the achievement of equality through service to the weak and the deprived.

Draft National Education Policy (1979) was put forward by the then Education Minister Pratap Chandra Chunder which proposed the development of such an educational system that would help the students not only to enhance their knowledge but also academic skills. It also called for building awareness of morals and ethics among students so that they can develop a good personality and become worthy citizens. It suggested for such an educational system that could reinforce the constitutional values. The thrust was on encouraging national integration through education. The basic features of this policy relating to secondary education were:

1. Organization of education at all levels would be the joint responsibility of the central and the state governments.
2. Individual efforts would be encouraged to organize education at any level, but the government would exercise control over every government and non-government educational institutions.
3. 8+4+3 would be implemented in the whole country.
4. The expansion of secondary education would be restrained and it would be improved qualitatively.
5. Secondary education would be of two types—general and vocational. The general education would prepare the students for higher education whereas the vocational secondary education would prepare them to earn their livelihood.

6. Curriculum of secondary education would be made utilitarian and more emphasis would be given on the practical knowledge rather than the theoretical knowledge.
7. Co-curricular activities would be given place in the curriculum of secondary level for the conservation of culture.
8. "Three language formula" would be implemented for the development of national integration.
9. Qualitative reform would be introduced in vocational and technical education.
10. Evaluative reforms would be given to students on the basis of their merits and economic conditions at any level of education.
11. Scholarship would be given to students on the basis of their merits and economic conditions at any level of education.
12. Special attention would be paid on the education of weaker sections of society.

National Policy on Education, (NPE–1986): The then Prime Minister of India Rajiv Gandhi stated, "Education in India stands at the cross-road today. Neither normal linear expansion nor the existing pace and nature of improvement can meet the need of the situation. It should be therefore re-examined and reorganized". Following this a survey of the existing system of education was conducted and was published in August 1985 entitled "Challenge of Education: A Policy Perspective". In this document the statistical description of the progress of Indian education from 1951 to 1985, areal picture of its achievements and failures, and a correct analysis of its merits and demerits were presented. The government made this document public and started a nationwide debate on it. Suggestions were received from different regions of the country. On the basis of these suggestions the central government prepared a new education policy and presented it in 1986, which is known as National Policy on Education, 1986. The basic features of National Policy on Education (1986) relating to the secondary education were:

1. Administration of education would be decentralized.
2. Sufficient resources would be made available for the organization of education at all levels.
3. 10+2+3 pattern of education would be implemented in the whole country.
4. Secondary education would be reorganized. At the secondary level, "three language formula" would be implemented and the education of mathematics, science, social science, history, nationalism, constitutional responsibility, citizen rights and duties, cultural heritage, and work experience would be made compulsory. Further, to achieve the objectives of secondary education, National Policy on Education (1986) had formulated following core elements for school curriculum:
   (a) History of India's freedom movement
   (b) Constitutional obligations
   (c) Nurturing the national identity
   (d) Preservation of cultural heritage
   (e) Caving of democratic set up
   (f) Equality of sexes
   (g) Protection of environment
   (h) Removal of social barriers
   (i) Sense of small family norms
   (j) Inculcation of scientific temper
5. Examination system and evaluation process would be uplifted.
6. Jawahar Navodaya Vidyalaya (JNV) would be established in every district to act as a model for other schools.
7. At the +2 stage, along with the general education, region specific vocational education would be provided.
8. Educational technology would be used for education at all levels.
9. Education would be made universally available through the means of mass communication.

10. Concrete steps would be taken for the equality of educational opportunity.
11. Special attention would be given to the education of the scheduled caste and scheduled tribe children, children of backward class and backward region, children of minorities, handicapped and mentally retarded children, and girls.

Janardhana Reddy Committee (1992): With respect to the implementation of National Policy on Education (1986), Ramamurti Committee (1990) presented its report in September, 1990. Again, in 1992, the government formed a new committee to review the implementation of this policy under the chairmanship of Janardhana Reddy. The committee observed that the secondary education boards, at that time, were unable to perform their work properly. It suggested to reorganize them and make them autonomous. It also suggested devolving administrative and financial power to the principals of secondary schools. It also stated about the expansion of open education at the secondary level. It placed special emphasis on the inclusion of vocational courses in the curriculum of secondary level and also to provide computer education at this level. At +2 stages, vocational stream should be strengthened and for this the higher secondary schools should be enriched with all the facilities. The committee suggested continuing of the Jawahar Navodaya Vidyalaya plan and opening more JNVs in remaining districts as soon as possible but at the same time it suggested to reform their entrance examination and working system.

Programme of Action (POA-1992): In 1992, the government of India amended the National Policy on Education (1986) along with its plan of action and proclaimed it as the Programme of Action, 1992. The amendments made relating to secondary education were:

1. Emphasis would be placed on the enrolment of girls, SCs, and STs children in the secondary education.
2. A 'National Evaluation Organization' would be formed for the reform in examination and evaluation.

3. Population education would be emphasised more in the primary and secondary educations.
4. More than six percent of the national income would be spent on education.
5. An examination reform framework would be prepared to provide guidance to the examining bodies.

National Curriculum Framework (NCF–2005): The Executive Committee of National Council of Education Research and Training (NCERT) had taken the decision, at its meeting held on 14th and 19th July 2004, to revise the National Curriculum Framework for School Education (NCFSE–2000) in the light of the report, *Learning Without Burden* (1993). In this context, a National Steering Committee, chaired by Prof. Yash Pal, and 21 National Focus Groups were set up. The NCF (2005) provides the framework for making syllabi, textbooks, and teaching practices within the school education programmes under the NCERT.

The main points under NCF (2005) for the secondary education are:

1. To train children to look after their health and develop it.
2. To provide children knowledge about different subjects and make them proficient in thinking, imagination, and decision making.
3. To socialize children and prepare them to bring about necessary social change.
4. To provide children knowledge of different cultures and develop cultural tolerance among them.
5. To inculcate social, cultural, moral, and national values among the children and guide them to behave accordingly; and develop their character and morality.
6. To guide children to do some physical work according to their interest, ability, and need.
7. To provide children knowledge about principles of democratic system of government and train them in democratic way of living.

8. To make children aware about the national goals such as conservation of environment and population control and develop among them scientific attitude, national integration, and feelings of internationalism.
9. To provide children general information about the main religions of the world and develop religious tolerance.

The Draft National Education Policy (2019): Drawing inputs from the T.S.R. Subramanian Committee report and the Ministry of Human Resource Development (MHRD), the K. Kasturirangan Committee has produced the policy document aiming to universalize the pre-primary education by 2025 and provide foundational literacy/numeracy for all by 2025. Now, the policy document is out in the public domain for discussion and comments. The policy aims at making India a knowledge superpower by equipping students with the necessary skills and knowledge. It also focuses on eliminating the shortage of manpower in Science and Technology, academics, and industry. The draft policy is built on foundational pillars of Access, Equity, Quality, Affordability, and Accountability.

The key features of the Draft National Education Policy are:

- The policy covers school education, higher education, and professional education. It aims to universalize the pre-primary education by 2025 and provide foundational literacy/numeracy for all by 2025.
- It proposes new curricular and pedagogical structure, with 5+3+3+4 structure covering the children in the age group of 3–18 years. Under this, Foundational Stage consists of Pre-Primary and Grades 1–2, and it looks at discovery learning and learning by play. The foundational literacy and numeracy skill is a mission mode approach under this policy that includes national tutors' program, remedial instructional aid programmes, etc. The next stage is Preparatory Stage that consists of Grades 3–5 for the children in the age group of 8–11 years followed by the Middle Stage consisting of Grades 6–8 for the children in the

age group of 11–14 years and the Secondary Stage consisting of Grades 9–12 for children in the age group of 14–18 years. This is an academic restructuring only, there will be no physical restructuring of schools.

- It also looks at the verticals of vocational education by including teacher education and the research and innovation.
- It aims at universal access and retention with 100 percent gross enrolment ratio for all school education by 2030.
- A 'three-language formula' has been proposed since children of age group 2–8 years learn languages most quickly and multilingualism has great cognitive benefits for students.
- The policy also tries to focus on certain foundational skills that children should have in the proposed new structure of 5+3+3+4.
- It proposes the creation of a new independent State School Regulatory Authority (SSRA).
- It proposes to constitute Rashtriya Shiksha Aayog or the National Education Commission, the apex body. It will be chaired by the Prime Minister and will comprise eminent educationists, researchers, Union Ministers, representative of Chief Ministers of States, and eminent professionals from various fields.
- MHRD will be re-designated as the Ministry of Education (MoE).
- The school education will cover children of age group 3–18 years, instead of the present 6–14 years under the RTE Act. It will cover three years under Early Childhood Care and Education (ECCE) and four years under secondary education. ECCE will facilitate play and discovery-based learning for children of that age group.
- The policy focuses on online learning as an alternative to regular classroom interaction between teachers and

students. It helps in achieving the twin objectives of cutting costs and increasing enrolment.

- It aims to protect and promote culture through the study of classical languages, mother tongues, and regional languages.
- The teacher education system will be transformed with rigorous preparation through a four-year integrated stage and subject-specific programs offered in multi-disciplinary institutions.

Objectives of NEP:

1. Expanding early childhood education for the age group of 3–5 years to ensure smooth transition to primary education.
2. Universal elementary and secondary education.
3. Equitable access to higher education.
4. All education programmes to be made accessible, inclusive, and responsive.
5. Elimination of social, regional, and gender gaps.
6. Promotion of skill development and vocational skills.
7. Reform in higher education system in order to ensure equitable access to tertiary education.
8. Integration of ICT in education.
9. To ensure all youths and at least 90 percent of adults achieve literacy numeracy skills prescribed by adult education programme.

Many commissions and committees have given their views regarding the structure and function of Secondary Education in India right from Secondary Education Commission–1952 till NPE–1986. Many changes have undergone in the society of 21st century. In this context, Secondary Education has also to address the changes taking place in the society in its curriculum, approach, transaction, objectives, and implementation of the programme according to the prospective NEP–2019, which is going to be implemented very soon.

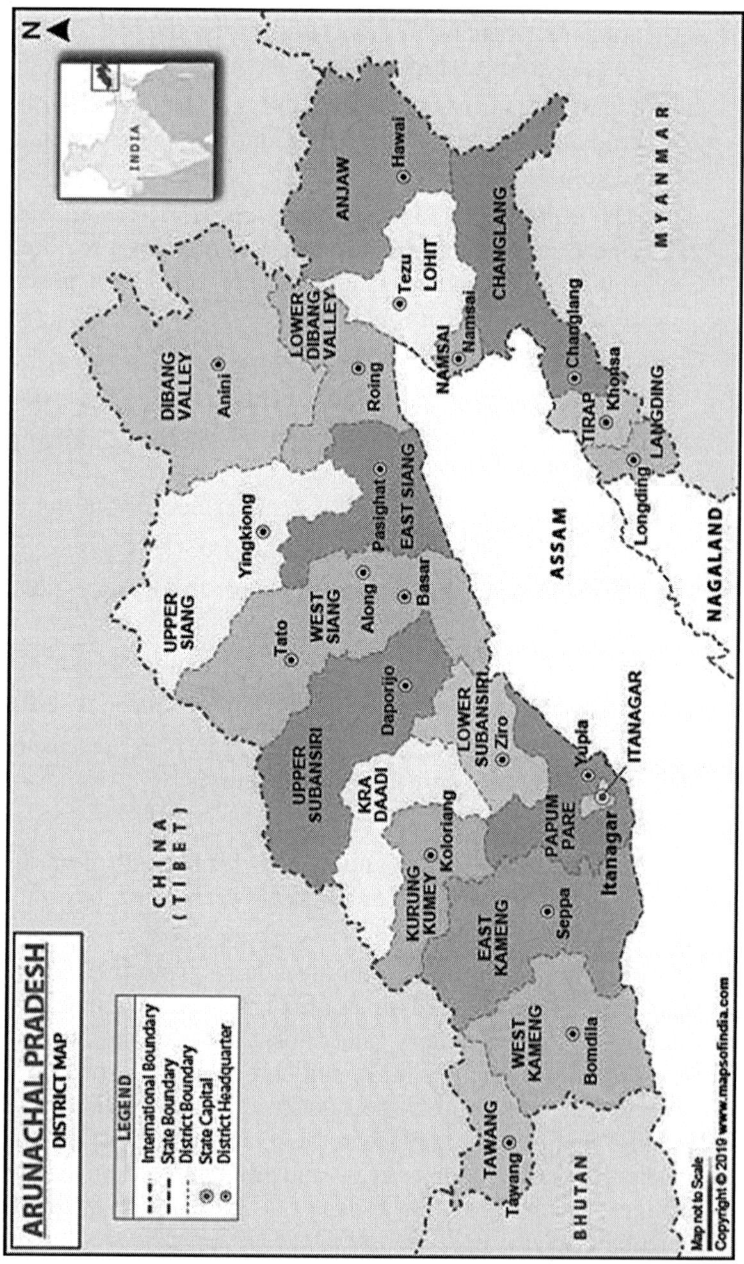

Figure 1.1: Map of Arunachal Pradesh

Educational Scenario in Arunachal Pradesh

Arunachal Pradesh, the land of rising Sun, is located in the North-Eastern part of the Indian Territory. It is a beautiful state in the North-Eastern lower Himalaya. It is the 24th state of India which spreads over an area of 84000 sq. km. It is situated between 26.28° N and 29.33° N latitude and 91.20° E and 97.30° E longitude. It has a long international border with China to the North and North-East, Myanmar to the East, and Bhutan to the West. It is the largest state in area in the Northeast region. Before 1972, it was known as North Eastern Frontier Agency (NEFA) under the Assam constituency. The name Arunachal Pradesh was coined and given by Bibhabasu Das Shastri, the then Director of Research, and K.A.A. Raja, the then Chief Commissioner of Arunachal Pradesh on 20th January, 1972, and inaugurated by the then Prime Minister of India, Indira Gandhi at Ziro, district headquarters of the Lower Subansiri district of Arunachal Pradesh. It was only on 20th February, 1987 that Arunachal Pradesh got the status of 24th fully fledged state of the Union of India, inaugurated by Rajiv Gandhi at Itanagar, the capital of the state.

As on April, 2021, Arunachal Pradesh has twenty-five districts, namely Anjaw, Changlang, Dibang Valley, East Kameng, East Siang, Kra Daadi, Kurung Kumey, Kamle, Lohit, Longding, Lower Dibang Valley, Lower Subansiri, Lepa Rada, Namsai, Papum Pare, Pakke-Kessang, Shi-Yomi, Siang, Tawang, Tirap, Upper Siang, Upper Subansiri, Upper Dibang Valley, West Kameng, and West Siang. The names of these districts are based on the names of famous rivers flowing through the respective districts. Arunachal Pradesh is one of the most sparsely populated states of India having the population of 13,82,611 according to 2011 census, scattered over 26 towns and 3863 villages.

In Arunachal Pradesh there are 26 major tribes and more than 100 sub-tribes belonging to Indo-Mongoloid racial stock. Most of the tribes inhibiting the land are ethnically similar, having derived from original common stock but their geographical isolation from each other has brought amongst them certain distinctive characteristics in language, dress, and customs. Each tribe has very rich culture and traditions. Also,

Arunachal Pradesh is the most linguistically diverse state and its languages belong to Tibeto-Burman language group. There are around 90 languages spoken in the state (G.N. Devy, Chairperson of People's Linguistic Survey, 2013).

The state of Arunachal Pradesh is endowed with rich and unique flora and fauna. There are eight wildlife sanctuaries, one orchid sanctuary, and two national parks in the state covering an area of 9,488,48 sq. km. Two national parks Namdapha and Mouling cover areas of 1985 sq. km. and 483 sq. km., respectively. Wildlife sanctuaries and orchid sanctuary in the state include Daying Ering, Dibang, Eaglenest, Kamlang, Kane, Mehao, Pakke, Tale Valley, and Sessa Orchid. Among the great variety of wild life, the most commonly noticed are tiger, black panther, leopard, wild elephant, barking deer, musk deer, monkey, wild buffalo, wild goat, flying fox, fruit-bat, etc. A strange creature, known as *takin* (Budorcas), can be seen in the regions of Siang district. Around 500 species of orchids are found in Arunachal Pradesh.

Table 1.1: District wise population, sex ratio, area, and literacy rate of Arunachal Pradesh (2011)

District	Population	Sex Ratio	Area (Sq. Km.)	Literacy (%)
Tawang	49,977	714	2085	59
West Kameng	83,947	819	7422	67.07
East Kameng	78,690	1028	4134	60
Papum Pare	1,76,573	980	3462	68.55
Upper Subansiri	83,448	998	7032	63.96
West Siang	1,12,274	930	8325	66.5
East Siang	99,214	980	4005	72.54
Upper Siang	35,320	889	6590	60
Changlang	1,48,226	926	4662	59.8
Tirap	1,11,975	944	2362	52.2
Lower Subansiri	83,030	984	3460	74.3
Lower Siang**	---	---	---	---
Lepa Rada**	---	---	---	---
Kamle**	---	---	---	---
Kurung Kumey	92,076	1032	6040	48.8

District	Population	Sex Ratio	Area (Sq. Km.)	Literacy (%)
Dibang Valley	8,004	813	9129	64.1
Lower Dibang Valley	54,080	928	3900	69.1
Lohit	14,5726	912	5212	68.2
Anjaw	21,167	839	6190	56.5
Longding**	---	---	---	---
Pakke Kessang**	---	---	---	---
Namsai**	---	---	---	---
Kra Daadi**	---	---	---	---
Siang**	---	---	---	---
Shi Yomi**	---	---	---	---
Total	13,83,727		938	65.4

Source: North-East General Knowledge, O.P. Gupta, Ramesh Publishing House (2019)

** These districts were created after 2011.

According to 2011 census, the literacy rate of Arunachal Pradesh was 65.4 percent whereas Lower Subansiri had the highest literacy rate of 74.3 percent and Kurung Kumey had the lowest literacy rate of 48.8 percent. As per the report of Unified District Information System for Education (UDISE), 2014–15, Arunachal Pradesh has the literacy rate of 65.38 percent and it possesses 415 secondary schools with the total enrolment of 53.67 percent. The gross access ratio at the state level is 52.74 percent which is lower than the national average of 71.46 percent.

The spread of education has brought many positive changes in the life styles and habits of the people of Arunachal Pradesh. In the beginning of 20th century, the condition of the education system in the state was absolutely in traumatic condition. The literacy rate was below 1 percent in 1947. There were no schools in the whole region. In 1918, the first school was set up at Pasighat in East Siang. During 1952–53, there were only 67 lower primary schools and only one middle school in the whole region. However, with the attainment of the status of statehood in 1987, the progress and development in the state accelerated gradually. According to the Directorate of School Education,

Arunachal Pradesh, during 2009–10, there were 118 higher secondary schools, 195 secondary schools, 873 upper primary schools, and 1842 primary schools in the entire state. During 2014–15, the status of recognised educational institutions in the state increased to 139 higher secondary schools, 228 secondary schools, 1122 upper primary schools, and 2228 primary schools. At present, the number of educational institutions is quite remarkable in the region.

Background of Rashtriya Madhyamik Shiksha Abhiyan (RMSA)

The RMSA was launched in March, 2009 by the Government of India with an objective to enhance access to secondary education and improve its quality. The scheme envisages to enhance the enrolment at secondary stage by providing a secondary school within reasonable distance of every habitant. The other objectives include improving quality of education imparted at secondary level by making all secondary schools conform to prescribed norms, removing gender, socio-economic and disability barriers, and providing universal access to secondary level education.

In order to meet the challenges of Universalisation of Secondary Education (USE), there is a need of a paradigm shift in the conceptual design of secondary education. The guiding principles in this regard are: Universal Access, Equality and Social Justice, Relevance and Development, and Curricular and Structural Aspects. Universalisation of secondary education gives opportunity to move towards equality. The concept of 'common school' will be encouraged. If these values are to be established in the system, all types of schools including unaided private schools have to contribute towards Universalisation of Secondary Education (USE) by ensuring adequate enrolment for the children from under privileged society and Below Poverty Line (BPL) families.

Goals and Objectives of RMSA

1. To ensure that all secondary schools have physical facilities, staff, and supplies according to the prescribed standard in the RMSA norms with special emphasis

on achieving and sustaining a pupil/teacher ratio of 30, pupil/classroom ratio of 40, adequate and fully equipped laboratories, computer rooms, and libraries.

2. To provide full financial support in case of Government, Local Body, and Government aided schools; and also encourage Public Private Partnership (PPP) of various kinds and extent with NGOs and private providers of education.
3. To improve access to secondary schooling to all children according to norms—through proximate location of secondary schools within 5 kms and higher secondary within 7 to 10 kms; and safe transport arrangements/ residential facilities, depending on local circumstances.
4. To ensure that no child is deprived of secondary education of satisfactory quality due to poverty, gender, socio-economic, disability, and other barriers.
5. To improve quality of secondary education through appropriate curriculum development, learning methodology, and teachers' training.

Achievement of the above goals and objectives would also, inter alia signify substantial progress in the direction of the Common School System.

Approach and Strategy for Universalizing Secondary Education

The strategy of universalizing access to secondary education and improving its quality are described below:

Access: There is a wide disparity in schooling facilities in different regions of the country. There are disparities between private and government schools as well as among the private schools. For providing universal access to quality secondary education, it is imperative that specially designed broad norms are developed at the national level and provision may be made for each state/union territories but also, wherever necessary, of the locality.

The norms for secondary schools in states should be developed in the pattern of Kendriya Vidyalayas run by Government of India. Development of the infrastructure facilities and learning resources are to be carried out in the following ways:

- Expansions/strategy of existing secondary schools and higher secondary schools shift in existing schools.
- Up gradation of upper primary schools based on micro planning exercise with all necessary infrastructure facilities and teachers. Ashram schools to be given preference while upgrading upper primary schools.
- Up gradation of secondary schools to higher secondary schools based upon the requirements.
- Opening of new secondary schools/higher secondary schools in unserved areas based on the school mapping exercise. All these buildings having mandatory water harvesting system and disabled friendly.
- Rain harvesting systems to be installed in existing school buildings also.
- Existing school buildings to be made disabled friendly.
- New schools also to be set up in public-private partnership mode.

Quality

- Providing required infrastructure like black board, furniture, libraries, laboratories for science and mathematics, computer labs, toilet clusters, etc.
- Appointment of additional teachers and in-service training of teachers.
- Bridge course for enhancing learning abilities for students passing out of elementary education.
- Reviewing curriculum to meet the National Curriculum Framework (NCF)–2005 norms.
- Residential accommodation for teachers in rural and difficult hilly areas. Preference to be given for accommodation of female teachers.

Along with improving the quality, RMSA has pressed upon promotion of the science laboratories, environmental education, yoga, vocational education, centrally sponsored schemes of population education project, international mathematics, and science Olympiads. Rashtriya Avishkar Abhiyan (RAA) has been implemented for improving teaching-learning of science and mathematics to cater quality resources.

Equity

- Free lodging/boarding facilities for students belonging to SC, ST, OBC, and minority communities.
- Hostels/residential schools, cash incentives, uniform, books, and separate toilets for girls.
- Providing scholarships to meritorious/needy students at secondary level.
- Inclusive education be the hallmark of all the activities. Efforts to be made to provide all necessary facilities for the differently abled children in all the schools.
- Expansions of Open and Distance Learning needs to be undertaken, especially for those who cannot pursue full time secondary education, and for supplementation/ enrichment of face-to-face instruction.

It is important to mention here that RMSA not only emphasizes on providing secondary education for the special focus groups that includes scheduled tribe and scheduled caste, minority girls, and children with special needs, but also it gives importance on removing the existing disparities in socio-economic and gender background in the secondary level of education by setting up secondary level schools at certain distance of the habitation or the feeder schools.

Samagra Shiksha Abhiyan (SSA)/Integrated Scheme of School Education (ISSE) in Arunachal Pradesh

Samagra Shiksha Abhiyan was started in Arunachal Pradesh on 1st April 2018 with the vision to ensure inclusive and equitable quality education from pre-school to senior secondary stage in accordance with the Sustainable Development Goal (SDG) for Education, which requires, by 2030,

- Ensuring all girls and boys complete free, equitable, and quality primary and secondary education leading to relevant and effective learning outcomes.
- Ensuring all girls and boys have access to quality early childhood development, care, and pre-primary

education so that they can be ready for primary education.

- Ensuring equal access for all women and men to affordable and quality technical, vocational, and tertiary education, including university.
- Eliminating gender disparities in education and ensuring equal access to all levels of education and vocational training for the vulnerable, including persons with disabilities, indigenous people, and children in vulnerable situations.
- Ensuring all learners acquire the knowledge and skills needed to promote sustainable development, including, among others, through education for sustainable development and sustainable lifestyles, human rights, gender equality, promotion of a culture of peace and non-violence, global citizenship, and appreciation of cultural diversity and of culture's contribution to sustainable development.
- Building and upgrading education facilities that are child, disability, and gender sensitive and provide safe, non-violent, inclusive, and effective learning environments for all.

This scheme focuses on two more areas such as Teacher and use of Technology for delivery of quality education.

Major Components of Samagra Shiksha Abhiyan

The major components of Samagra Shiksha Abhiyan are: universal access including infrastructure development and retention; gender and equity; inclusive education; quality; financial support for teachers' salary; digital initiatives; Right to Education entitlements including uniforms, textbooks, etc.; pre-school education; vocational education; sports and physical education; strengthening of teacher education and training; monitoring; programme management; and national component.

A successful programme of Universalisation of Elementary Education (UEE) is the precondition for taking the first reliable step towards Universal Secondary Education. The NPE emphasised improving equitable access to secondary education and the enrolment of girls, SCs, and STs, particularly in science, commerce, and vocational streams (Para 5.13 of the NPE, 1986). The NPE and the Programme of Action (POA), 1992 while recognising secondary education as a critical instrument for social change, called for its planned expansion. The NPE, (as modified in 1992) specifically laid emphasis again on increasing access to secondary education with particular focus on participation of girls, SCs, and STs; increased autonomy of Boards of Secondary Education to enhance their ability to improve quality; introduction of ICT in school curriculum for coping with globalisation; renewed emphasis on work ethos and values of a humane and composite culture in the curricula; and vocationalisation through specialised institutions or through the refashioning of secondary education to meet the manpower requirements of the growing Indian economy (Para 5.13 to 5.15). The Rashtriya Madhyamik Shiksha Abhiyan (RMSA) scheme initiated in 2009, demonstrated the government's ambition for a secondary education system that can support India's growth and development. In the year 2013-14, four other Centrally-sponsored Schemes for secondary education viz., ICT in Schools, Girls' Hostel, Vocationalisation of Secondary and Senior Secondary Education and Inclusive Education for Disabled at Secondary Stage (IEDSS) were subsumed under RMSA. This was done to provide for convergence based implementation of different programmes for secondary education with inclusion of aided schools for quality related interventions and senior secondary segment for certain components.

The Integrated Scheme on School Education envisages the 'school' as a continuum from pre-school, primary, upper primary, secondary to senior secondary levels. The vision of the Scheme is to ensure inclusive and equitable quality education from pre-school to senior secondary stage in accordance with the Sustainable Development Goal (SDG) for Education.

The major objectives of the Scheme are:

- Provision of quality education and enhancing learning outcomes of students;
- Bridging social and gender gaps in school education;

- Ensuring equity and inclusion at all levels of school education;
- Ensuring minimum standards in schooling provisions;
- Promoting Vocationalisation of education;
- Support states in implementation of Right of Children to Free and Compulsory Education (RTE) Act, 2009;
- Strengthening and up-gradation of State Councils of Educational Research and Training (SCERTs)/State Institutes of Education (SIE) and District Institute of Education and Training (DIET) as nodal agencies for teacher training.

The main outcomes of the Scheme are envisaged as Universal Access, Equity and Quality, promoting Vocationalisation of Education, and strengthening of Teacher Education Institutions (TEIs).

The scheme is committed to provide universal access to quality education at secondary and senior secondary stage. With a view to facilitating States/UTs, the scheme provides support in establishment of new schools by up-gradation of upper primary school to secondary schools and up-gradation of secondary schools to senior secondary schools and, thus, for establishment of composite schools. The scheme also supports for strengthening existing schools. The first priority would be strengthening of existing schools, then, provision of additional sections in the existing schools, and then up-gradation of existing upper primary to secondary as well as secondary to senior secondary schools. Opening of new standalone schools should be the last priority, to be done as an exceptional measure only in un-served areas.

Achievements under Samagra Shiksha in Arunachal Pradesh

- 342 pre-primary in existing schools, 1666 primary schools, 713 upper primary schools, 81 secondary schools, 154 residential schools, 12 hundred bedded and 42 fifty bedded hostels in existing government upper primary schools, 4 hundred bedded residential hostels at secondary level, and 48 Kasturba Gandhi

Balika Vidyalayas have been opened and made functional.

- 4602 primary teachers, 2248 upper primary teachers including 34 head teachers, 433 subject teachers including 81 head masters in secondary schools, and 430 part time instructors in upper primary schools have been recruited so far under samagra shiksha.
- 99 Block Resource Centres and 1 Urban Resource Centre have been strengthened with permanent building and support staffs including Resource Persons for different subjects and CWSN and MIS coordinators, data entry operators, and accountants for academic support to the teachers and the schools.
- 5758 additional classrooms, 2106 boys and 3280 girls' toilets, 315 CWSN toilets, drinking water facilities in 1874 schools, boundary walls in 1068 schools, electricity in 626 schools, 869 ramps with handrails, 313 handrails in existing ramps, major repairs of 1392 primary schools, 200 bedded girls hostel at secondary level, 199 type-II residential quarters. 172 computer rooms, 154 library rooms, 171 Art/Craft rooms, and 151 science laboratories have been completed. 180 primary schools and 269 upper primary schools have been facilitated with head masters' rooms. Besides, ICT has been facilitated in 229 secondary and higher secondary schools.
- Out of School Children (OoSC) have dropped down to 932 from 74213 since inception of Samagra Shiksha Abhiyan. Special Training Package for OoSC has been developed and distributed to the districts. State is committed to mainstream OoSC through residential and non-residential special training.
- An updated and improved version of Unified District Information System for Education (UDISE) known as UDISE+ (plus) has been introduced in 2018-19 for collection of data online in real time and data has been collected for the year 2018-19.

- 5861 in-service elementary teachers both regular and contractual, sponsored by SSA for acquiring professional qualification as per National Council for Teacher Education (NCTE) norms complying the RTE act, have successfully passed out 2 year D.El. Ed. through ODL mode of IGNOU. Besides, 3577 untrained elementary teachers including 652 Govt. school teachers appeared in D.El.Ed and 375 B.Ed holder primary teachers appeared in the Professional Development Programme for Elementary Teacher (PDPET) Examination through NIOS in the month of March 2019.
- National Achievement Survey (NAS) has been conducted successfully for all subjects for the classes III, V, and VIII in 2017 under SSA.
- The guidelines on-class and subject-wise Learning Outcomes for all elementary classes have been given to all the teachers, and training has been imparted to resource persons. State is committed to ensure intensive training to all the teachers on Learning Outcomes, and identify all the children with less than grade level learning competencies for providing learning support, so that all children reach the desired grade—appropriate competency level.
- Orchid Series, a supplementary Graded reader containing 30 folktales each for classes I and II of 13 major tribes and III–V of 16 major tribes of Arunachal Pradesh have been developed and introduced in all the primary schools in the form of reading corners targeting the children for development of their language skills. A supplementary graded reader containing folktales of 16 major tribes targeting the children of classes VI–VIII has been developed.
- Teachers and students diary for elementary have been developed to provide each and every teacher and student at elementary level.

- Under innovation Exposure Visit within and outside the state for meritorious students of elementary schools and quiz competition under innovation and RAA also were conducted in the districts.
- Science and Maths Clubs have been introduced in 100 Govt. Schools with highest class upto VIII across the state under Rashtriya Avishkar Abhiyan (RAA) through UNISED.
- 2962 Early School Mathematics Kits for classes I and II, 390 Primary English Language Kits (Raindrop), and 1019 each of Science and Mathematics Kits for classes VI–VIII developed by NCERT have been provided to Govt. Primary and Upper Primary Schools in the state.
- Biometric enabled Tablets to all Govt. Schools and Computer Sets to 99 BRCs and 1 URC have been provided in all over state.
- Composite School Grant and grants for academic support through BRCs/CRCs in addition to textbook, uniform, maintenance, and stipend for the boarders of Residential Schools and KGBVs released to the districts.
- Nistha under National Initiative for School Head and Teacher Holistic Advancement training for 100 KRPs and 20 SRPLs have already been conducted, and batch wise training for 1433 elementary teachers including head teachers, BRCCs, and CRCCs is in progress across the state.

Enhancing quality of school education requires systemic reform for translating the vision of quality in this Scheme into the lived experience of all children in the schools. However, making significant improvements to system-wide educational outcomes is a complex task that requires a multi-faceted approach. Not a single element is sufficient for progress, all are necessary. At the core are policies and guidelines that focus on improving teaching and learning, including curriculum, teaching skills, leadership, and assessment. However, at the time of implementation, plans by the States/UTs must take into account the context and possibilities for implementation by referring the guidelines on quality parameters. These may be followed up with appropriate executive instructions and training to all stakeholders.

An Overview of the Review of the Related Literature

The present study is an attempt to investigate and measure the development and problems of secondary education in the state of Arunachal Pradesh. In this section, major studies related to the concerned area along with a conceptual framework of secondary education have been reviewed, because a review of related literature serves as a tool to examine various aspects that a researcher needs to be mindful and also clarifies which areas to be focused and the areas to be avoided. Therefore, some of the important reviews on secondary education and the related literatures have been considered in this study. A wealth of research findings indicates that the conditions and management of secondary education is not very satisfactory due to lack of infrastructures, lack of finance, overcrowded classes, poverty of parents, unfavourable conditions at home, poor enrolment, etc., (Bhaipal, 1984; Mishra, 1983; Jala, 1987; Langstieh, 1989).

A study made by *Mohanti* (2007) revealed that enormous increase in number of students in secondary institutions affected the quality of secondary education. It indicates that the major causes of students' failure were lack of basic resources, academic atmosphere, professional commitment of teachers, academic guidance, and monitoring and evaluation system.

Finn, Gerber, and Boyd-Zaharias (2005) observed that poor academic achievement throughout the school year was related to students leaving school without graduating.

Nakopodia (2010) found that student dropout was common at secondary stage and male dropout was more than that of female dropout. *World Bank Report on Secondary Education in India* (2009) points out that at the secondary level, the enrolment rates are far more unequal than those at the primary level. The secondary education enrolment by gender shows a persistence ten-point difference over the last ten years between boys having enrolment of 45 percent and girls having enrolment of 35 percent. The gender equity issues become more acute when ratios are disaggregated at the state level. Several northern states stand out as most inequitable at the secondary level.

Biswal (2011) made a study on *Secondary Education in India: Development Policies, Programmes, and Challenges.* The study indicates that the growth rate of secondary level institutions during the period has remained much lower compared to that of the middle level. It may be underlined that, at the all India level, during the period 2000/01 to 2007/08, the average annual growth rate of enrolment at secondary and higher secondary stage was highest (7.06%) compared to that of the middle (4.23%). At the all India level, the Gross Enrolment Ratio (GER), which shows total enrolment in secondary state as a percentage of the total population in the relevant age group also increased steadily from 19.3% in 1990/91 to 44.81% in 2007/2008. Among the major states, only Tamil Nadu and Kerala had relatively higher level of participation in secondary education with a GER of more than 75% in 2007/08.

Nyokir, A. (2011) had a study on the *Status of Secondary School Education in Arunachal Pradesh: A Critical Study.* The study found low academic performance among the students of four selected districts in secondary education, indicating insufficient necessary infrastructure facilities, lack of transportation facilities, and problems in fund management in the schools.

Matthew (2013) did a study on *Provision of Secondary Education in Nigeria: Challenges and Way Forward.* The study reveals the following challenges that are plaguing secondary education in Nigeria and undermining the achievement of its objectives: inadequate fund, inadequate and decay of infrastructural facilities, inadequate and low quality teachers, negative attitudes of teachers, indiscipline of students, low quality intakes and poor academic performance of students, prevalence of examination malpractice, incidences of wastages, inappropriate curriculum, and dilemma of disarticulation of schools.

World Bank (2013) put India as an "underperformer" in secondary education. "Secondary education hasn't received the attention it deserves, when compared with elementary and higher secondary levels (in India)," Sam Carlson, Lead Education Specialist, World Bank. The report noted 40 percent gap in secondary enrolment rates between students from the highest and lowest expenditure quintiles. While there is 20 percent difference in enrolment for secondary education in urban and rural areas, a persistent gap of 10 percent exists between boys and girls. The report states that uneven distribution of school infrastructure, lack of trained teachers, inefficient teacher deployment, sub-optimal use of private sector in expanding enrolment capacity and insufficient schooling opportunities are hurting India's progress. It also mentions that 27 percent of India's districts have less than one secondary school for every 1000 students in the age group of 15 to 19.

Singh, T.T. (2016), in his study *A Study of the Management Problems of Un-aided Private Secondary Schools of Manipur*, found that the private un-aided schools do not get any financial grant from the government. They have to generate revenue using their own resources. The school authorities of the private un-aided schools have to face many problems in running the schools and one of them is related to the lack of trained subject teachers as it is observed that professionally trained teachers are not available. In spite of all these problems, these schools yield better results and they also solicit the involvement of community and parents in their management systems.

The study of *Tarannum* (2016), "A study of administrative behaviour of Heads and work motivation of teachers in relation to their perception of total quality management of secondary schools" concludes that the variables of age and teaching experience have some effects on the total quality management of the secondary schools. Female teachers are high on perception of total quality management and administrative behaviour compared to male teachers. Besides, the finding shows that the effect of administrative behaviour and total quality management on work motivation and the relationship is significant and positive. Therefore, it concludes that administrative behaviour can be an important factor in motivating employees in an organization, especially in secondary schools.

Dalchandra (2018) conducted a study on “An Empirical study of school management for quality education in Southern Rajasthan”, which reveals that age group plays a significant role in sample distribution but no significant difference is observed in terms of management in government and private schools.

Various similar studies in this field were conducted by researchers in the past. Some of the studies were conducted in primary and higher secondary levels; and some were conducted in different states and countries encompassing problems and development of education. In the rapidly changing multidimensional scenario of Arunachal Pradesh in particular and India in general, forced by the global concern for improving the quality of education to cope up with the challenges of the changing scenario in times ahead, the above discussed studies have shown that lots of researches have been conducted in India and abroad relating to the various quality dimensions of secondary education but hardly any research has been taken up in Arunachal Pradesh relating to development and problems of the secondary education except the study conducted by *Nyokir, A.* (2011) on status of secondary school education in Arunachal Pradesh. Therefore, to explore this area of knowledge, this project has been taken up with the expectations that the findings will immensely be helpful for the educational administrators, planners, teachers, parents, and community for getting feedback and improving the quality of secondary education in Arunachal Pradesh.

Rational of the Study

Secondary education plays a crucial role in the formal schooling system as it is the gateway for higher education and also a link to the job market. Since secondary education along with elementary education is the backbone of every nation's education system, to make this stage of education successful and relevant to the society, there is a need to provide quality education at this stage, which will make balance between continued learning and the world of employment. The key elements on which the quality education depend are student’s performance, teacher’s performance, evaluation procedures, adherence to time frames, and infrastructure supports in achieving the set goals.

The present study intends to provide a comprehensive picture on the development and problems of secondary education. It is felt that in spite of its great value for the development process as per the secondary education policies and schemes, the performance of secondary education has been far from satisfactory in its implementation. Like in other states, the system of education in Arunachal Pradesh is also based on the education policy of the Nation. However, there are some variations in the educational structure within the school stage. Programmes like Sarva Shiksha Abhiyan (SSA) and Rashtriya Madhyamik Shiksha Abhiyan (RMSA) have been launched in the State of Arunachal Pradesh in the year 2001 and 2010, respectively. Secondary Education in Arunachal Pradesh has lots of shortcomings. The dropout rate is alarming at the secondary level. Tirap and Upper Siang districts have highest dropout rates of 12.65% and 10.7%, respectively, which require special attention and intervention. The Gross Access Ratio at the state level is 52.74% which is lower than the national average of 71.46%.

Since the last few years, the state has not reported the conduction of in-service training. Under Inclusive Education for Disabled at Secondary Stage (IEDSS), no special educator has been recruited in the state due to lack of availability of qualified special educators as per the scheme. There is a lack of adequate number of trained teachers who are the actual disseminators of knowledge. Under Sarva Shiksha Abhiyan (SSA), appointments of teachers are made on ad-hoc basis. Teachers recruited under this scheme are mostly not dedicated to education of students, and they remain absent from the schools due to delayed disbursement of their salary and lack of quarter accommodations near the schools where they are posted. Such untrained and unmotivated teachers truly cannot provide quality education to students who need a strong foundation of knowledge.

Most of the secondary schools in the interior rural areas do not have electricity connection which prevents teachers from using modern devices like computer for teaching and management of schools. In the 21st century, lack of infrastructure is a serious challenge and will not let the schools as well as the education system grow to their fullest potential which is a matter of great concern.

Continuous and Comprehensive Evaluation (CCE), introduced in all the government schools in 2010, has caused a major setback in the quality of education in Arunachal Pradesh. It can be observed that none of the stakeholders have understood the concept of CCE. Till 2017 session, students were awarded grades and promoted to next class without continuous observation and assessment which has affected the quality of education as well as the products of the system.

Therefore, it is imperative to explore the problems of Secondary Education in order to facilitate such discussions that will provide light for the policy makers, stakeholders, and state educational authorities to give a serious concern to the performance of secondary education system in Arunachal Pradesh. The investigator has taken appropriate steps to conduct a thorough study on the development and problems of Secondary Education in Arunachal Pradesh.

Statement of the Problem

A study on the development and problems of Secondary Education in the state of Arunachal Pradesh.

Operational Definitions of the Term Used

- **Secondary Education:** The education that a child receives after elementary education and before higher education. It begins at age 11 to 13 and ends at age 15 to 16. Government and Private Secondary 10th grade schools come under it.
- **Academic Achievement:** A measure of knowledge gained in formal education usually indicated by test scores, grade points, average, and degree. In simple term, it refers to the performance of 10th grade students in their previous examinations.
- **Information Communication Technology (ICT):** It is defined as diverse set of technological tools, devices,

and resources used to communicate, and to create, disseminate, store, and manage information for the purpose of learning.

- **ICT Access:** The availability and opportunity to use of information communication technology equipments, devices, and software resources as part of learning by secondary school students.
- **Attitude:** Attitude of Secondary School Students towards the Secondary Education.

Objectives of the Study

The objectives formulated for the study are:

(i) To examine the Development of Secondary Education in the State of Arunachal Pradesh from 1947 to 2017.

(ii) To investigate the Enrolment, Promotion, Repetition, and Dropout rates of Students at the Secondary Stage of Selected Districts.

(iii) To explore the Administrative set up for the functioning of Secondary Education.

(iv) To investigate the availability of infrastructure facilities in Secondary Schools.

(v) To examine the Academic Achievements of Secondary School Students of Arunachal Pradesh.

(vi) To compare Academic Achievements of 10th grade students of Arunachal Pradesh before and after the removal of CCE Pattern of Evaluation.

(vii) To find out the Problems faced by Principals/ Headmasters, Teachers, and Students at Secondary Education in Arunachal Pradesh.

(viii) To study the Attitude of Secondary School Students in Arunachal Pradesh towards Secondary Education with regard to management.

(ix) To investigate the role of State Government Officials towards the development of Secondary Education in Arunachal Pradesh.

Research Questions

The research questions framed for the study are:

(a) How is the development of Secondary Education in Arunachal Pradesh?

(b) What is the status of Secondary School in Arunachal Pradesh?

(c) Is the enrolment at Secondary School stage satisfactory?

(d) How is the Administrative set up for the functioning of Secondary Education?

(e) Are the infrastructural facilities available in Secondary Schools?

(f) Is the academic performance satisfactory at Secondary level?

(g) Is there any difference in academic performance of male and female students?

(h) How is the teaching conducted in Secondary Schools?

(i) What is the medium of instruction in Secondary Schools?

(j) What are the effects of Continuous and Comprehensive Evaluation?

(k) Are the teachers trained in Secondary Schools?

(l) What are the problems of Secondary Education in the State?

(m) How is the attitude of students regarding Secondary Schools?

Hypothesis of the Study

The following hypothesis has been formulated according to the nature of the present study:

H01: There exists no significant difference in the Attitude between the Government and the Private Secondary School Students towards Secondary Education.

Delimitations of the Study

The research design of the present investigation has certain delimitations which are briefly mentioned below.

1. The present study is delimited to the sample groups of Secondary educational institutions under general stream, which are affiliated to Board of Secondary Education, Arunachal Pradesh.
2. The study is delimited to 10th grade Secondary School students of Arunachal Pradesh.
3. The study has been delimited to twenty districts of Arunachal Pradesh.

2
Methodology

Introduction

The methodology in an educational research describes the steps and procedures adopted by the researchers in a particular study. Travers (1958) observes that Educational research represents an activity directed towards the development of an organized body of scientific knowledge about the events with which educators are concerned. Koul (2009) states "Research is an objective, impartial, empirical, and logical analysis and recording of controlled observations that may lead to the development of generalizations, principles or theories, resulting to some extent in prediction and control of events that may be consequences or causes of specific phenomena". Thereby, methodology is a part of research activity which speaks of procedures followed in true sense in an educational research work. Based on these assumptions, an attempt has been made to present a systematic procedure carried out in this study.

Research Design and Method Adopted in the Present Study

The research design is a framework of techniques and methods which are suitable for the undertaken study. It is adopted by the researchers by looking into the appropriateness of the study undertaken. It is considered as a step by step process of any research work. It maintains a logical sequence and is designed in a logical manner corresponding to the way in which research is expected to be carried out. It defines various types of study such as historical, descriptive, experimental, and so on.

The present study is based on the prevailing conditions and aimed at obtaining precise and clear information regarding the current status of the development and problems of secondary education in the state of Arunachal Pradesh. Besides, in support of this, normative survey method is important to be adopted. Therefore, by keeping in view its significance, the researcher has adopted normative survey method of descriptive studies.

Selection of The Districts

The present study has been undertaken in the twenty districts of Arunachal Pradesh and included districts are Anjaw, Changlang, Dibang Valley, East Kameng, East Siang, Kra-Daadi, Kurung Kumey, Lohit, Longding, Lower Dibang Valley, Lower Subansiri, Namsai, Papum Pare, Siang, Tawang, Tirap, Upper Siang, Upper Subansiri, West Kameng, and West Siang. The remaining five districts of Kamle, Shi-Yomi, Lower Siang, Pakke Kessang, and Lepa Rada were not included in the study as they were created recently. Since, these districts were bifurcated from the old districts, the objectives in which secondary data have been used, considers these districts as well.

Table 2.1: Districts included in the present study

Arunachal Pradesh			
↓	↓	↓	↓
Anjaw	Changlang	Dibang Valley	East Kameng
East Siang	Kra-Daadi	Kurung Kumey	Lohit
Longding	Lower Dibang Valley	Lower Subansiri	Namsai
Papumpare	Siang	Tawang	Upper Siang
Upper Subansiri	Tirap	West Kameng	West Siang

Table 2.2: The list of Selected Schools in Arunachal Pradesh

Sl. No.	Name of the Government Schools	Sl. No.	Name of the Private Schools
1.	Government Town Secondary School, Yingkiong	1.	Royal Siang Academy, Jengging
2.	Government Rijo Secondary School, Upper Subansiri	2.	Royal Siang Academy, Yingkiong
3.	Government Secondary School, Kapu	3.	Pinewood School, Khonsa

Sl. No.	Name of the Government Schools	Sl. No.	Name of the Private Schools
4.	Government Higher Secondary School, Pongchau	4.	St. Joseph English School, East Kameng
5.	Government Higher Secondary School, Longding	5.	Don Bosco School, Longding
6.	Government Secondary School, Etalin	6.	Light of the World, Miao-town
7.	IGJ Government Higher Secondary School, Pasighat	7.	Siang Model School, Pasighat
8.	Government Higher Secondary School, Mechuka	8.	St. Xavier's International School, Aalo
9.	Government Higher Secondary School, Kaying	9.	St. Joseph's High School, Kaying
10.	Government Secondary School, Mayu	10.	Intaya Public School, Roing
11.	Government Secondary School, Hayuliang	11.	Vivekananda Kendra Vidyalaya, Amliang
12.	Government Secondary School, Manhofa	12.	Pine Dale Public School, Bomdila
13.	Government Secondary School, New Seppa	13.	Green View School, Namsai
14.	Government Secondary School, RGU Campus	14.	Good Shepherd Public School, Pappu Nallah
15.	Government Secondary School, Nirjuli	15.	Kingcup Public School, Itanagar
16.	Government Secondary School, Yazali	16.	St. John Bosco School, Yachuli
17.	Government Higher Secondary School, Ziro	17.	Bluepine Residential English School, Hapoli
18.	Government Higher Secondary School, Nyapin	18.	Don Bosco School, Kra-Daadi
19.	Government Higher Secondary School, Kra-Daadi	19.	Calvary English School, Kurung Kumey
20.	Government Town Secondary School, Tawang	20.	Tawang Public School, Tawang
Total	20	Total	20

Interpretation: Some of the schools are situated in the interior areas of the state but all the twenty districts of Arunachal Pradesh have been covered while collecting the data for the present study. The data were collected from twenty government secondary schools and twenty private secondary schools situated in various districts of Arunachal Pradesh. Thus, total 40 secondary schools both from government and private sectors have been covered in this study.

Description of Population of the Study

In an educational research, a sample is drawn from the population which is interchangeably termed as universe. The research population is a group/collection of individuals, subject, object, institution, or a geographical area which are selected by a particular researcher for the study. Generally, it is well defined having similar characteristics as the selected population has common characteristic or traits which may include age, gender, locality, management, class, etc. Therefore, the population of study is a group of individual or phenomena selected completely based on the personal choice of the researcher for a particular study.

The population in the present study have been taken from the twenty selected districts of Arunachal Pradesh and include all the education officers, headmasters/principals, teachers, and students of Government and Private Secondary Schools.

Sample and Sampling Procedure

A sample is a representative group of the total population in an undertaken study and is drawn from the population or universe. It is thereby a group of individuals, people, subject, object, institution, or a geographical area taken out of the selected population as a representative picture. It represents larger population/universe by bearing all the characteristics of the universe or population for the purpose of observation and analysis by which a researcher generalizes the findings of the study. The sampling technique is the process or technique of drawing out sample from the larger population to be put in a particular study.

According to the requirements of the present study, the stratified random sampling technique of probability sampling technique has been used. Using this sampling technique, the investigators have selected forty government and private secondary schools along with four groups of individuals having similar characteristics. They are: (a) Fifteen government education officers from different districts of Arunachal Pradesh. The education officers related to the Secondary Education are District Deputy Director of Secondary Education (DDSE), Block Resource Coordinator (BRC), Block Education Officer (BEO), State Project Coordinator (SPC), and District Project Coordinator (DPC). (b) Forty headmasters/principals from the selected schools were included. (c) 589 government and private secondary school teachers from the selected schools of the twenty selected districts were included in the sample. (d) Finally, 2083 10th grade students were selected both from government and private schools of the selected districts. It included students studying in government secondary schools, government higher secondary schools having 10th grade, and schools managed by private ownership having 10th grade.

The sampling process is shown below:

Table 2.3: The Sampling Process of the Government Education Officers in the Present Study.

Arunachal Pradesh
↓
20 Districts
↓
15 Education Officers

Interpretation: The above figure indicates the selection of fifteen Educational Officers from the twenty selected districts of Arunachal Pradesh. Educational Officers included are DDSE, BRC, BEO, SPC, and DPC. They were selected from the districts of Papum Pare, West Kameng, East Kameng, Upper Siang, East Siang, Tirap, Tawang, Changlang, Upper Subansiri, Kurung Kumey, Lower Dibang Valley, and Longding. The Educational Officers were selected to investigate the problems and development of the secondary education in the state.

Table 2.4: The Sampling Process of the Headmasters/ Principals in the Present Study.

Arunachal Pradesh	
↓	
20 Districts	
↓	↓
Government	Private
↓	↓
20 Headmasters/ Principals	20 Headmasters/ Principals

Interpretation: The above figure indicates the selection of headmasters/principals from the twenty selected districts of Arunachal Pradesh. Twenty headmasters/principals were selected from government secondary schools and twenty from the private secondary schools of selected districts. All the selected twenty districts were touched for drawing this sample group.

Table 2.5: The Sampling Process of the Secondary School Teachers in the Present Study

Arunachal Pradesh	
↓	
20 Districts	
↓	↓
Government	Private
↓	↓
319 Secondary School Teachers	270 Secondary School Teachers

Interpretation: The above figure indicates the selection of secondary school teachers from twenty selected districts of Arunachal Pradesh. The sample includes teachers who were working at various government and private secondary schools. It includes 319 teachers from government secondary schools and 270 from private secondary schools. The total sample of teachers in this study is 589.

Table 2.6: The Sampling Process of the Secondary School Students (particularly 10th grade) in the Present Study.

Arunachal Pradesh	
↓	
20 Districts	
↓	↓
Government	Private
↓	↓
1213 Secondary School Students	870 Secondary School Students

Interpretation: The above figure indicates the selection of secondary school students from selected schools of selected districts of Arunachal Pradesh. The sample includes students from government secondary schools, government higher secondary schools having 10th grade, and private higher secondary schools. Total 1213 students (particularly 10th grade) were selected from government secondary schools and 870 from private secondary schools of selected districts of Arunachal Pradesh. The total sample of students in this study is 2083.

Criteria Adopted while Selecting the Sample

For obtaining a generalised and reliable result, a well defined set of criterion were adopted while selecting the sample for the study. The criterion followed for the sample collection are:

(a) **Coverage of the Districts:** As per the initial research proposal, only ten districts of Arunachal Pradesh were to be covered in this study. But, attempt had been made to cover all the districts of the state and finally twenty districts were covered out of twenty-five districts because five districts were created during the process of the study. Since, all the newly created districts were curved out of the old districts, more or less they were covered indirectly in this study.

(b) **Population and Sample of the Present Study:** The population and sample in the present study differs district wise in terms of its total number/population. The fifteen selected government Education Officers were not selected from all the selected districts of the state. Most of the Education Officers were taken from the Directorate of Secondary Education head office at Papum Pare. However, all the twenty selected districts were covered while drawing sample for headmasters/ principals, teachers, and students. According to the proportion of the population in a particular district, samples were drawn for headmasters/principals, teachers, and students. For instance, Papum Pare district is the most populated district in the state, so the highest number of samples were drawn from this district. Likewise, Dibang Valley is the least populated district and thereby, lowest number of samples were drawn from this district.

(c) **Sampling Technique:** The present study adopted stratified random sampling technique in order to give equal chance of selection to all the headmasters/ principals, teachers, and students in the selected twenty districts of the state.

(d) **Variables:** The variables for the study were Gender (Male and Female), Management (Government/ Private), and Year (2013-2018).

(e) **Main Focus:** The main focus of the study was to analyse the problems and development of secondary education in Arunachal Pradesh. To investigate the problems and development, both primary and secondary data were taken from U-DISE sources at Secondary Education Office, and from education officers, headmasters/ principals, teachers, and students through interview schedule and questionnaires.

Table 2.7: The Independent Variables of the Study and the Distribution of Government Education Officers

Education Officer						
Gender		Community		Professional Qualification		Designation and Nos.
M	**F**	**Tb**	**NT**	**T**	**UT**	DDSE – 7, State Project Coordinator – 1, District Project Coordinator – 2, BEO – 4, BRC – 1
14	1	15	0	15	0	

Note: M = Male, F = Female, Tb = Tribal, NT = Non-Tribal, T = Trained, UT = Untrained.

Interpretation: Fifteen Education Officers related to the Secondary Education were selected from the different districts of Arunachal Pradesh and they were interviewed. Out of the fifteen government Education Officers, there were 7 DDSE, 1 SPC, 2 DPC, 4 BEO, and 1 BRC.

Table 2.8: The Independent Variables of the Study and the Distribution of Headmasters/Principals

Gender		Community		Management		Professional Qualification	
M	**F**	**Tb**	**NT**	**G**	**P**	**T**	**UT**
30 (15 G, 15 P)	10 (5 G, 5 P)	25 (18 G, 7 P)	15 (3 G, 12 P)	20	20	39 (20 G, 19 P)	1 (0 G, 1 P)

Note: M = Male, F = Female, Tb = Tribal, NT = Non-Tribal, G = Government, P = Private, T = Trained, UT = Untrained.

Interpretation: The above table displays the selected headmasters/principals from various districts of the state. The sample contained 40 headmasters/principals, out of which 30 were male taken from 15 government and 15 private secondary level schools and 10 were female from 5 government and 5 private secondary schools. Considering the community variable, there were 25 tribal headmasters/principals from 18 government and 7 private secondary schools and 15 non-tribal from 3 government and 12 private secondary schools. The sample included 20 government and 20 private secondary school headmasters/principals. Out of the 40 headmasters/principals,

39 were trained and only 1 was untrained who belonged to the private secondary school. Out of 39 trained headmasters/principals, 20 were from government and 19 were from private secondary schools.

Table 2.9: The Independent Variables of the Study and the Distribution of Teachers

Teachers							
Gender		Community		Management		Professional Qualification	
M	**F**	**Tb**	**NT**	**G**	**P**	**T**	**UT**
309	280	301	288	319	270	447	148

Note: M = Male, F = Female, Tb = Tribal, NT = Non-Tribal, G = Government, P = Private, T = Trained, UT= Untrained.

Interpretation: The above table shows the distribution of selected teachers according to the independent variables under study. The sample contained 589 secondary school teachers, out of which 309 were male and 280 were female; 301 were tribal and 288 were non-tribal; 319 were from government and 270 were from private secondary schools; and 447 were trained and 148 were untrained.

Table 2.10: The Independent Variables of the Study and the Distribution of Students

Students							
Gender		Community		Management		Settlement	
B	**G1**	**Tb**	**NT**	**G**	**P**	**R**	**U**
1006	1077	1513	570	1213	870	600	1483

Note: B = Boys, G1 = Girls, Tb = Tribal, NT = Non-Tribal, G = Government, P= Private, R = Rural, U = Urban.

Interpretation: The above table shows the distribution of selected students according to the independent variables under study. In order to compare the status of development and problems of secondary schools, the students were selected both from government and private secondary schools. The rest of the variables were not used specifically in the present study but the details are mentioned here simply for the general information. The sample included 2083 secondary school students, particularly 10th grade, out of which 1006 were boys and 1077 were girls; 1513 were tribal and 570 were non-tribal; 1213 were from government secondary schools and 870 were from private secondary schools; and 600 were from rural areas and 1483 from the urban areas of the state.

Research Tools Used

The present study uses both primary and secondary sources of data. For primary sources, interview schedule and four questionnaires were constructed and used, whereas some government data were used as secondary sources. Government sources were used to investigate enrolment and academic achievement of 10th grade secondary school students of Arunachal Pradesh during 2013–2018, number of government and private secondary schools during 2013–2018, number of secondary school teachers during 2013–2018, and dropout, repetition, and promotional rate of the secondary school students during 2013–2018. The interview schedules were arranged for the Education Officers in order to collect information regarding problems and development of Secondary Education in Arunachal Pradesh. The questionnaires were given to headmasters/principals, teachers, and students of government and private secondary schools of the state. These questionnaires were self developed for investigating the development and problems of Secondary Education in the state. The following are the details of the tools used by the researchers for collection of the data.

1. Primary Sources

(a) Interview Schedule:

- Interview Schedule for the Government Education Officers.

(b) Questionnaires:

- Problems of the Head-in-Charge of Secondary Schools in Arunachal Pradesh (2018),
- Problems of Secondary School Teachers in Arunachal Pradesh (2018),

- Problems of Secondary School Students of Arunachal Pradesh (2018) and,
- Attitude Scale for Secondary School Students towards Secondary Education (2018).

2. Secondary Sources (U-Dise Sources from School Education Office)

- Enrolment and Academic Achievement of 10th grade students,
- Number of Secondary Schools in Arunachal Pradesh (government and private),
- Number of Secondary School Teachers in Arunachal Pradesh (government and private),
- Dropout, Repetition, and Promotion rates of the 10th grade students in Arunachal Pradesh.

Description of the Tools (Primary Sources)

A. Interview Schedule

The researcher framed some questions for interview schedule beforehand to be put before the Government Education Officers of various districts. The interviewed officers included 7 DDSE, 4 BEO, 2 Project Officers, 1 State Project Coordinator, and 1 BRC. There were 21 unstructured questions for the Education Officers relating to the development and problems of secondary education in the state. Questions that were framed for investigating the problems of secondary education in the state included the areas relating to programmes that were not functioning well as per the Secondary Education Policy in Arunachal Pradesh, problems regarding posting of teachers, rules for duration of posting, ratios for each secondary school, whether the authority faced hindrance/political pressure at the time of recruitment of teachers, problems while selecting quality/ skilled teachers, action taken by the state authority against absentee teachers, steps taken to stop back door entry during recruitment of teachers, sharing some points on provision to stop encroachment of schools' boundary land. sharing of how to take the matter of some defunct schools in the state observed after the declaration of CBSE results, and sharing of some points on the problems of secondary education in Arunachal Pradesh.

Regarding the development of the Secondary Education in Arunachal Pradesh, there were some unstructured questions framed beforehand which covered the areas, such as RMSA programme functioning as per the policy guidelines, sharing of some of the state policy programmes which were effectively implemented for the quality enhancement of the Secondary Education, status of the existing infrastructure facilities in the schools, indicating the status and feasibility of infrastructure facilities provided to the schools by the state government, i.e., buildings/rooms, furnitures, classrooms/blackboards, fans, laboratory rooms, library with books, sport items, computer rooms, and teachers. Some questions were related to having separate grievance redressal cell for the secondary education in the state, satisfactory release of funds to the institution in the state, proper utilization of funds, organization of inspection visits to the secondary schools, selected members of the inspection team, scholarships provided to the students by education department, satisfaction with the present performance/result of the secondary schools, keeping of records of the private schools by the state government, provision for vocational education in secondary schools of the state, and suggesting some ways to improve the present education system.

B. Questionnaire

i. *Problems of the Head-in-Charge of Secondary Schools in Arunachal Pradesh (2018)*

It is a self developed tool by the researcher in the form of a questionnaire framed particularly for the present study to investigate the problems of Secondary Education as well as the status of infrastructure facilities in Arunachal Pradesh in 2018. A set of 49 different types of questions was prepared. Questions included in the set were question for "Yes" and "No", tick (√) the correct option, and inviting suggestions from the headmasters/ principals/head-in-charge on various issues. The questionnaire was provided with the proper instructions which explained that one could tick one or more options given in a particular question, should avoid abbreviations and confusing remarks, had no time limit to complete the questions, and should answer all the questions with utmost sincerity.

Table 2.11: Sections of the Questionnaire for Head-in-Charge

SECTION	DESCRIPTION
A	Infrastructure
B	Teacher
C	Curriculum, Co-curricular Activities, Teaching-Learning, and Evaluation
D	Management, Finance, and Supervision

Interpretation: The questionnaire was divided into four sections. In Section-A, questions were related to the infrastructure; Section-B included questions related to the teachers; Section-C consisted questions on curriculum, co-curricular activities, teaching-learning, and evaluation; and Section-D had questions on management, finance, and supervision.

In Section-A, questions on infrastructure included the areas, such as: whether the school has its own land and building, type and structure of school building, availability of sufficient playground and boundary wall, road connectivity, hostel facilities for students, sufficient furniture, physical conditions of the classrooms like desk and benches, blackboard/whiteboard, fans, electricity, and whether properly ventilated. Questions were also related to facilities such as auditorium, teachers' quarters, principal's office, staff room, EDUSAT/internet connectivity, smart classrooms, computer rooms, store room, laboratory facilities, availability of audio-visual aids, school library, drinking water facility, separate toilet for both boys and girls, first-aid facility, and ramp/railing facility for physically challenged students.

In Section-B, questions on teacher included the areas, such as: number of school teachers (both male and female), whether teachers are sufficient in number, whether number of science teachers are sufficient, teachers' punctuality and commitment towards their profession, teachers using teaching-learning materials/teaching aids, and whether the school have skilled manpower like computer teacher, music teacher, sports teacher, NCC/Scouts and Guide teacher, and yoga teacher.

In Section-C, questions on curriculum, co-curricular activities, teaching-learning and evaluation included the areas, such as: satisfaction with the existing curriculum as per National Curriculum Framework for School Education (NCFSE), 2005; whether existing curriculum relevant, productive, conceptual, and up-to-date; whether syllabus of secondary grade relevant; whether present curriculum includes hard sports; difficulties in the implementation of Rashtriya Madhyamik Shiksha Abhiyan (RMSA) scheme; problems in organizing co-curricular activities; whether schools take students to field trips and excursion; whether students' attendance and academic performance satisfactory; mostly used medium of instruction by teachers; frequency of assessment of students in the schools; most appropriate evaluation system for teachers' attainment and holistic learning of students; main examination and evaluation problems and suggestions to be provided by head-in-charge on improvement of examination and evaluation system.

In Section-D, questions on management, finance, and supervision included the areas, such as: support of School Management Committee (SMC) members; schools having institutional planning; holding of staff meeting in a month; financial sources of schools; maintaining of records like teachers' attendance, students' register, admission register, Cumulative Record Card (CRC) of students, staff meeting record, Parent Teacher Association (PTA) meeting register, and store log book. This section also included questions on preparation of school budget, annual audit of school accounts, financial assistance to schools, inspection of schools, problems regarding school management, and suggestion to be taken for improvement of school management.

Table 2.12: Problems of the Head-in-Charge of Secondary Schools in Arunachal Pradesh and its Item Distribution.

Section	Description	"Yes" or "No"	Tick (√) Correct Option	Opinion Based/ Suggestion	Total No. of Item/ Question
A	Infrastructure	12	5	0	17
B	Teacher	3	4	0	7
C	Curriculum, Co-curricular Activities, Teaching-Learning, and Evaluation	9	3	1	13
D	Management, Finance, and Supervision	4	7	1	12
Total		28	19	2	**49**

Interpretation: The questionnaire contains 49 items/ questions. Section-A contains 12 Yes/No type questions and 5 choice based questions related to infrastructure. Total number of questions in this section is 17. Section-B contains 3 Yes/No type questions and 4 choice based questions related to teachers. Total number of questions in this section is 7. Section-C contains 9 Yes/No type questions, 3 choice based questions, and 1 opinion/ suggestion based question related to curriculum, co-curricular activities, teaching-learning, and evaluation. Total number of questions in this section is 13. Finally, Section-D contains 4 Yes/ No type questions, 7 choice based questions, and 1 opinion/ suggestion based question related to management, finance, and supervision. Total number of questions in this section is 12.

i(a). Scoring

Since, the questions included in the questionnaire were not purely of one type and, also, they were not necessarily based on correct and incorrect options, the researchers simply indicated and included the positive response for particular question in one group and the negative on the other. Each appropriate and desirable answer was given a score of 1 and every inappropriate and undesirable answer was given a score of 0. Some of the questions included in the questionnaire were provided with more than two options and all the options were appropriate and valued. Therefore, in such questions, the respondent had the opportunity to score 3, 4, 5, 6, 7, and 8 based on the total number of options provided in a particular question. Thus, the questionnaire had total score of 76.

i(b). Reliability

The questionnaire was first given to 35 headmasters/ principals of secondary and higher secondary schools of Papum Pare district of Arunachal Pradesh for testing the reliability. After a gap of four weeks, it was again redistributed to them. The obtained scores of these subjects in both the cases were correlated which resulted the reliability coefficient of 0.78.

i(c). Validity

Along with the testing of reliability, the validity of the tool was also established through various means. The test had a validity score of 0.76.

ii. *Problems of Secondary School Teachers in Arunachal Pradesh (2018)*

It was a self developed tool in the form of questionnaire framed for the teachers to evaluate the problems as well as the infrastructure facilities of Secondary Schools/Education in the state of Arunachal Pradesh in 2018. It consisted of 44 different types of questions including questions for "Yes" and "No", tick (√) the correct option, and suggestions to be provided by the teachers on various issues. The questionnaire was provided with proper instructions which explained that one could tick one or more options given in a particular question, should avoid abbreviation and confusing remarks, had no time limit to complete the questions, and should answer all the questions with utmost sincerity.

Table 2.13: Sections of the Questionnaire for the Teachers

SECTION	DESCRIPTION
A	Teaching Profession
B	Infrastructure
C	Academic, Curriculum and Evaluation
D	Management and Administration

Interpretation: The questionnaire was divided into four sections. Section-A consisted of questions related to the teaching profession, Section-B related to infrastructure, Section-C related to academic, curriculum, and evaluation, and Section-D related to management and administration.

In Section-A, questions on teaching profession included the areas, such as: teachers' satisfaction with their teaching job, commitment towards teaching profession, punctuality in the school, following of the code of ethics of the profession, interest in seminar/conference/research work, awareness on RTE Act and its intervention, and undergoing training for RTE Act.

In Section-B, questions on infrastructure included the areas, such as: sufficient infrastructure in staff room, laboratory facility for science students, problems in using audio-visual aids/teaching aids, problems of the school library, adequate safe water drinking facility, separate toilet facility for boys and girls, and transportation services.

In Section-C, questions on academic, curriculum, and evaluation included the areas, such as: satisfaction towards existing curriculum as per National Curriculum Framework for School Education (NCFSE), 2005, text books whether relevant/ up-to-date/suitable to the needs of students, whether syllabus of secondary grade emphasis on skill based knowledge, completion of syllabus on time by teachers, difficulty in implementation of Rashtriya Madhyamik Shiksha Abhiyan (RMSA), satisfaction regarding attendance and students' performance, use of teaching-learning materials/teaching aids, familiarity to take classes through Computer Aided Instruction (CAI) or in smart classrooms, mostly used medium of instruction, most appropriate evaluation system, main examination and evaluation problems, and suggestions to be provided by teachers for the improvement of examination and evaluation system.

Finally, in Section-D, questions on management and administration included the areas, such as: cooperation and regularity of head-in-charge, leave of in-service training programme, grievances mechanism/anti-corporal punishment cell, collection of extra fees from students, expression of opinion before the authority by teachers, release of convergence grant, use of teaching skills, common problems observed among students, areas with most problems faced by teachers, holding of staff meeting, visiting of inspection team, reasons for deteriorating quality education in the secondary schools, maintaining records like Cumulative Record Card (CRC), admission register, store log book, Parent-Teacher-Association (PTA) meeting, staff meeting, science lab and time table, problems in organizing activities such as workshop/seminar, career counselling, sports events, field trips/excursion, literary events, assembly events, NCC/Scouts and Guides, and main problems and suggestion for the improvement of school management.

Table 2.14: Problems of Secondary School Teachers in Arunachal Pradesh and its Item Distribution.

Section	Description	"Yes" or "No"	Tick (√) Correct Option	Opinion Based/ Suggestion	Total No. of Item/ Question
A	Teaching Profession	5	2	0	7
B	Infrastructure	7	0	0	7
C	Academic, Curriculum, and Evaluation	7	5	1	13
D	Management & Administration	8	8	1	17
Total		27	15	2	**44**

Interpretation: The above table shows the distribution of 44 items/questions under different heads. Section-A contains 5 Yes/No type questions and 2 choice based questions related to teaching profession. Total number of questions in this section is 7. Section-B contains 7 Yes/No type questions related to infrastructure. Section-C contains 7 Yes/No type questions, 5 choice based questions, and 1 opinion/suggestion based question related to academic, curriculum, and evaluation. Total number of questions in this section is 13. Finally, Section-D contains 8 Yes/No type questions, 8 choice based questions, and 1 suggestion/opinion based question related to management and administration. Total number of questions in this section is 17.

ii(a). Scoring

Each appropriate and desirable answer was given a score of 1 and every inappropriate and undesirable answer was given a score of 0. Some of the questions in this questionnaire had more than 2 options and all the options were appropriate and valued. Therefore, in such questions, the respondent had the opportunity to secure 3, 4, 7, and 12, based on the total number of options provided in a particular question. This questionnaire carried the total score of 80.

ii(b). Reliability

For testing the reliability of the questionnaire, the prepared questions were given to a sample of 50 teachers of secondary and higher secondary schools of Upper Siang and Papum Pare districts of Arunachal Pradesh. After a gap of four weeks, the questionnaire was re-distributed to the same subjects. The obtained scores of these subjects in both the cases were correlated which resulted the reliability coefficient of 0.90.

ii(c). Validity

Along with the testing of reliability, the validity of the tool was also established through various means. The test had a validity score of 0.78.

iii. *Problems of Secondary School Students of Arunachal Pradesh (2018)*

It is a self developed tool in the form of questionnaire framed for the students in order to investigate the problems and infrastructure facilities of Secondary Education/Schools in Arunachal Pradesh in 2018. It consists of 25 different types of questions including questions for "Yes" and "No", tick (√) the correct option, and suggestions to be provided by the students on various issues. The questionnaire was provided with the proper instructions which explained that one could tick one or more options given in a particular question, should avoid abbreviations and confusing remarks, had no time limit to complete the questions, and should answer all the questions with utmost sincerity.

Table 2.15: Problems of Secondary School Students in Arunachal Pradesh and its Item Distribution.

"Yes" or "No"	Tick (√) Correct Option	Opinion Based/ Suggestion	Total No. of Item/ Question
12	12	1	25

Interpretation: The above table shows the number of items/ questions in the tool for secondary school students of Arunachal Pradesh. Unlike the questionnaire for head-in-charge and teachers, the questionnaire for students was not divided into sections, instead questions were divided into various types such as 'Yes' or 'No', marking the appropriate response(s), and suggestions/ opinion based. It had 25 questions regarding problems and infrastructure facilities of secondary schools/education. Out of the total 25 questions, 12 were to be responded in "Yes" or "No", 12 questions were to be responded by choosing/marking the appropriate answer(s), and only 1 question was on problem and suggestions based.

In this questionnaire, students were asked whether they attend the school regularly. Were they satisfied with teaching-learning process? Did they face difficulty in understanding lessons taught by their teachers? After which questions regarding physical condition of classrooms were included such as desk and benches, blackboard/whiteboard, fans, electricity, and classrooms ventilation. Questions based on the facilities available in the schools such as auditorium hall, playground, hostel facility, career counselling cell, EDUSAT/internet connectivity, computer room, and smart classrooms were also included. Besides, various questions were included in this questionnaire relating to laboratory facility, library, teachers' punctuality, presence of resource teachers (like computer teacher, music teacher, sport teacher, NCC/Scouts and Guides, yoga teacher, etc.), use of Teaching-Learning-Materials (TLM)/Teaching Aids by the teachers, most difficult subjects for students, safe drinking water facility, separate toilets, bus/transportation, service, Swacch Bharat Abhiyan, social discrimination, pressurize to play or sit with same gender, completion of syllabus and its relevance to the present context, various co-curricular activities organized in the schools, mostly used teaching method by teachers, medium of instruction, evaluation system, main problems faced by students at school and suggestions provided by them for betterment of their school.

iii(a). Scoring

Each appropriate and desirable answer was given a score of 1 and every inappropriate and undesirable answer was given a score of 0. Some of the questions in this questionnaire had more than 2 options and all the options were appropriate and valued. Therefore, in such questions, the respondent had the opportunity to secure 4, 5, 7, and 18 based on the total number of options provided in a particular question. This questionnaire carried the total score of 72.

iii(b). Reliability

For testing the reliability of the questionnaire, the prepared questions were given to a sample of 120 secondary school students of Papum Pare and Lower Subansiri districts of Arunachal Pradesh. After a gap of one month, the questionnaire was re-distributed to the same subjects. The obtained scores of these subjects in both the cases were correlated which resulted the reliability coefficient of 0.78.

iii(c). Validity

Along with the testing of reliability, the validity of the tool was also established through various means. The test had a validity score of 0.87.

iv. *Attitude Scale for Secondary School Students towards Secondary Education (2018)*

It is a self developed tool using Likert's Five Point Attitude Scale in the form of questionnaire framed for the students in order to investigate the attitude of students towards secondary school education. The Likert's Five Point Attitude Scale is a five response category scale with SA, A, U, D, and SD, where SA stands for Strongly Agree, A stands for Agree, U stands for Undecided, D stands for Disagree, and SD stands for Strongly Disagree. In this attitude test, respondents have to respond by choosing any of these options in all the statements provided. Generally, in such attitude scale, there are no right or wrong statements. Responses are based on the attitude of the respondents.

This scale consists of a combination of 27 different types of statements regarding attitude of students towards secondary school education. Before each statement, there is a direction given to the students for their responses. The direction included instructions such as "read the instructions carefully before filling the statements". It directs the students with the explanation that the purpose of the attitude scale is to seek their opinion relating to existing system of Secondary Education in Arunachal Pradesh.

Statements included in this scale covered the areas such as: sincerity and regularity of teachers in teaching-learning activities, dependence of Secondary Education on quality Primary Education, role of Secondary Education in ensuring proper mental development, receiving quality and value education, awareness of environmental problems among students/learners, support and encouragement of parents for children's education, role of school life in holistic development of personality, sense of good citizenship and dignity of labour, base for scientific studies, relevance of secondary school curriculum, community participation, cooperation of village education committee, management of time table, inspection, health habits, vocational education, parent-teacher-association meeting, creative thinking ability, continuous and comprehensive evaluation pattern, grading system, evaluation and examination, Rashtriya Madhyamik Shiksha Abhiyan (RMSA) scheme, separate institutional plan, and future employment of the students.

Table 2.16: Positive and Negative Statements on the Attitude Scale

Positive Statements	Negative Statements
1, 2, 3, 4, 5, 6, 7, 8, 9, 10, 12, 13, 14, 16, 17, 20, 21, 22, 23, 24, 25, 26, & 27	11, 15, 18, & 19

Interpretation: Out of the total 27 statements, only four statements were negative in nature and the rest of the statements were considered positive. As there exists no statement that can be considered right or wrong, all the statements are either positive or negative in nature. The above table indicates that only statements such as 11, 15, 18, and 19 are considered as negative statements. The rest of the statements such as 1, 2, 3, 4, 5, 6, 7, 8, 9, 10, 12, 13, 14, 16, 17, 20, 21, 22, 23, 24, 25, 26, and 27 are all considered as positive statements.

iv(a). Scoring

In this tool, every positive response gets a score of 1 and every negative response a score of 0. Therefore, this tool carries the total score of 27 as there are total 27 statements in this scale. Every student has the opportunity to score from 0 to 27 in this tool.

iv(b). Reliability

To check the reliability of the test, the test-retest method of reliability was used. Under this method, 120 secondary school students were given the structured questionnaire in the district of Papum Pare and Lower Subansiri. After a gap of two months, the same questionnaire was redistributed to the same subjects. The obtained scores of the subjects in both the cases were correlated which resulted the reliability co-efficient of 0.72.

iv(c). Validity

The validity of the statement for this tool was first determined by its face validity after which the content validity was checked by reading and analysing the contents and situations of secondary schools and students. After which, the item validity was computed using the co-efficient of reliability. The reliability index was computed which indicated high validity of 0.88. From the total number of 80 statements, the statements in this tool were reduced to 27 after the proper evaluation.

Description of the Tools (Secondary Sources)

Following data were obtained from the secondary sources.

(a) Enrolment and academic achievement of 10th grade students.

(b) Number of secondary schools (government and private) in Arunachal Pradesh.

(c) Number of secondary school teachers (government and private) in Arunachal Pradesh.

(d) Dropout, repetition, and promotion rate of the 10th grade students in Arunachal Pradesh.

The data on the enrolment and academic achievement of 10th grade students were obtained from the offices of Secondary Education located in Itanagar and Papum Pare. The enrolment of 10th grade students includes number of students who have taken admission during the academic sessions 2013–2018 in both government and private secondary schools. Likewise, academic achievement data shows the class X (matriculation) results of students studying in the government and private schools having 10th grade during the academic sessions 2013–2018.

The number of secondary schools in Arunachal Pradesh simply displays the total number of both government and private secondary schools existed during the academic sessions 2013–2018. Similarly, the number of secondary school teachers in Arunachal Pradesh displays the total number of both government and private secondary school teachers existed during the academic sessions 2013–2018.

The Dropout, Repetition, and Promotion rates of the 10th grade students in Arunachal Pradesh specifically show the numbers of secondary school students particularly 10th grade students who were dropped out of the respective schools or repeated the same grade in the next academic session or students who were allowed to promote after passing a particular grade/ standard and division at the end of the academic year.

Procedure for Data Collection

A systematic process was used to collect the data for the present study. Fifty secondary schools were visited for the purpose of data collection. Personal visits by the researchers along with the self-developed questionnaire were made to the sample schools of the twenty selected districts. The data were collected first from Papum Pare and West Kameng districts. From Papum Pare district, the total number of 4 Educational Officers, 2 Headmasters/Principals, 35 Secondary School Teachers, and 234 Secondary School Students were taken and included in the study sample whereas from West Kameng district, 1 Education Officer, 2 Headmasters/Principals, 23 Secondary School Teachers, and 76 Secondary School Students were included in the sample.

After the collection of data from the districts of Papum Pare and West Kameng, an attempt was made to collect the data from both government and private secondary schools of the districts of Tirap, Changlang, Lohit, Longding, Namsai, Anjaw, Dibang Valley, Lower Dibang Valley, Upper Siang, Siang, West Siang, East Siang, Lower Subansiri, Kurung Kumey, Kra-Daadi, Upper Subansiri, East Kameng, and Tawang. From these districts, respectively 24, 30, 35, 34, 28, 23, 19, 35, 30, 27, 35, 30, 37, 21, 25, 29, 35, and 34 Secondary School Teachers (Government and Private) were selected. The total number of selected Secondary School Teachers were 589. Similarly, 61, 95, 101, 83, 94, 84, 86, 100, 100, 84, 101, 128, 110, 103, 108, 112, 101, and 122 Secondary School Students (Government and Private) were taken respectively from the selected districts. The total number of secondary school students in the sample were 2083.

As mentioned earlier, 4 Government Education Officers were taken from Papum pare district and 1 from West Kameng district of the state. The rest of the Government Education Officers were taken from the districts of Upper Siang, East Siang, Tirap, Tawang, Changlang, Upper Subansiri, Lower Dibang Valley, East Kameng, Longding, and Kurung Kumey. The total number of Government Education Officers included in the sample were 15. Besides, from each selected districts two Headmasters/Principals, one from Government Secondary School and one from private Secondary School, were taken for the study. Thus, total 40 Headmasters/Principals were included in the sample of present study.

For administration of tools, Headmasters/Principals of each selected school were contracted personally with requisite documents such as letter of permission from the competent authority and identity card. They were told the importance of the present study and their cooperation was sought for the collection of required data. And then they were provided the questionnaire to be answered. In the case of teachers and students, permission was taken from the Head of respective institutions and when the permission for data collection was granted by the Principals/Head-in-Charge of the respective schools, the proper explanation of the purpose of visit was explained and the process of collection of data began. For teachers, generally, during the break time, the investigators had entered the staffs' room and the purpose of data collection was explained to them along with the instructions. Then, all the required questionnaires were distributed to them. The investigator remained in the staffs' room for the purpose of clearing various doubts in the questionnaires. This way the data were obtained in realistic and natural settings. Because of the busy schedules and heavy workload given to teachers, questionnaire was not filled completely. So teachers were requested to complete the responses in the questionnaire by holding some days but not more than 4 days. Therefore, the same schools were revisited for the purpose of receiving back the distributed questionnaires.

For collecting data from the students, researchers had to take the permission from the Head of the schools and sometimes from the respective teachers as well, because the data were to be collected during the school hours. All the students were explained the importance of research work as general and about the present work in particular. They were praised for their cooperation and in some cases some sweets were distributed to them. There were two tools constructed for them. One was to investigate problems and infrastructure facilities of secondary schools and the other was to study their attitude towards Secondary Education. All the questions and the statements were explained serially and systematically and along the way they were asked to fill the questionnaires. The data from students were collected on the same day.

In the case of Government Education Officers, the data could not be taken on the same day along with the data of headmasters/principals, teachers, and students. To get data from them, either their offices were visited or their personal residences were approached. With their agreement, time was fixed for personal interview at their chosen place. All the Government Education Officers were very cooperative and active in their participation in responding the unstructured questions asked to them during the interview. Not to mention that most of the headmasters/principals, teachers, and students were very cooperative while providing the required information for the present study.

Along with the above primary sources, some secondary data sources were used, such as Unified District Information System for Education (U-DISE). For collecting data on Enrolment and Academic Achievement of 10th grade students, number of Secondary Schools (Government and Private), number of Secondary School Teachers (Government and Private), and Dropout, Repetition, and Promotion rates of the 10th grade students in Arunachal Pradesh, the Director of Secondary Education was met and permission was taken from him to use the sources of the department. The Director of Secondary Education directed his officials to cooperate in the data collection process for the concerned study.

Scoring of the Collected Data

All the tools constructed for the present study have a systematic procedure of their own. They are either similar or dissimilar in nature. The tools constructed for Head-in-Charge, teachers, and students on problems and infrastructure facilities in secondary schools of Arunachal Pradesh bear similar characteristics, i.e., every desirable/appropriate answer has a score of 1 and every undesirable/inappropriate answer/response has a score of 0. Three of these tools also have more than 1 score in a particular question. There are three types of questions in the tools constructed for Head-in-Charge, teachers, and students on problems and infrastructure facilities such as Yes/No type, putting a tick (√) on the appropriate answer, and providing suggestions/opinion on some questions. In Yes/No type of questions, for every 'Yes' response, respondent was given a score of 1 and for every 'No' response, the respondent was given a score of 0. For putting a tick (√) on the appropriate answer, the respondent had the opportunity to score more than 1 in a particular question and for opinion/suggestion based questions, every desirable answer was given a score of 2. In all, in the tool constructed for Head-in-Charge, the respondents had the opportunity to score 76, 80 in the tool constructed for teachers, and 72 in the tool constructed for the secondary school students.

The Attitude Scale constructed for the secondary school students of Arunachal Pradesh has 27 statements. Its scoring procedure is simple as every positive response gets a score of 1 and every negative response gets a score of 0 based on the self-structured scoring procedure set by the researchers. Therefore, the participant secondary school students had the opportunity to score 27 in this tool.

Data Treatment and Statistical Techniques Employed

The researchers had used appropriate statistical techniques for the analysis and interpretation of data and for formulation of objectives and hypotheses for the study. Some of the statistical techniques used in the present study are:

- Percentage,
- Mean,
- Standard Deviation, and
- T-test.

Conclusion

Methodology explains all the steps and procedures adopted by the researchers in every study while conducting a research work. In the current chapter, the investigator has presented methodology of the educational research which included the research design, method adopted, selection of the districts, description of the population, sample and the sampling procedure, and description and criteria adopted while selecting the sample for the study. Besides, tools used were depicted and described properly. The procedure of data collection, scoring, and statistical techniques used were also explained in this chapter.

3

Analysis and Interpretation

Introduction

Analysis and interpretation of data is a pivotal process in every research activity without which a research work is considered incomplete. It is the process which aims at delivering important information regarding what has been done with the collected data from the sample. It gives the real sense and meaning to the data which assists in generalization of the results in a particular study undertaken by the researcher. In order to present original work, researcher in the present study collected both primary and secondary data and subjected them to statistical techniques such as percentage, mean, standard deviation, and t–test. Later, based on the formulated objectives and the hypotheses, the collected data were classified and tabulated.

The secondary data on academic achievement of 10th grade students, enrolment of students in secondary schools, number of teachers and schools, and the dropout, repetition, and promotion rates among the 10th grade students were collected from the Office of School Education using U-DISE (Unified District Information System for Education). Whereas, for the primary data, 50 government and private secondary schools were selected out of which 40 Principals/Headmasters, 589 secondary school teachers, and 2,083 10th grade students were taken in the sample. Besides, out of the selected twenty districts, 15 Government Education Officers were drawn for the sample. The primary data were gathered in order to study the problems, development, and infrastructure facilities in the secondary schools of Arunachal Pradesh.

By looking into the necessity of the present study and in accordance with the formulated objectives and hypotheses, the researchers have proceeded to write the analysis and interpretation of the collected data in an appropriate and systematic manner.

Analysis and Interpretation of the Development and Problems of Secondary Education in Arunachal Pradesh

Objective I: *To examine the development of Secondary Education in the state of Arunachal Pradesh from 1947 to 2017.*

In the field of educational development, Arunachal Pradesh has not inherited any educational system of its own rather it follows the system of education which is prevailing in other parts of the country. The history of educational development is of great significance from the stand point of understanding the nature of educational activities. The land of Arunachal Pradesh was hidden and neither the ancient nor the medieval education had any sign of influence here before 1947. Being the late starter in the field of education in the year 1918 at Pasighat, the state remained backward as compared to other part of Northeast Region and another school was opened by Adi Community of Dibang Valley in 1922 at Dambuk. But, there is a record of some other schools which were established before 1947 such as Ningroo (1934), Boleng (1940), Riga (1940), Balk (1946), Yomcha (1947), Along (1947), Pasighat (1947), etc. In all these schools, the medium of instruction was Assamese during those days. It indicates that there was no much educational development before and even after independence and the pace of educational development was very slow. Arunachal Pradesh (before 1972, known as North-East Frontier Agency) had 67 Lower Primary Schools (LPS) and one Middle School (MS) with 120 teachers at LPS level and 6 teachers at MS level. The number of students at LPS and MS levels were 2674 and 34, respectively. In the year 1955-56, there were 152 Lower Primary Schools, 16 Middle Schools, and 3 Secondary Schools in the whole of the state and the literacy rate was recorded below 1.0 percent. In the year 1963-64, there were 179 Lower Primary Schools, 25 Middle Schools, and 7 Secondary and Senior Secondary Schools with 359,141, and 113 teachers by having 7200, 2267, and 1306 students, respectively. It shows that the pace of educational development was not satisfactory in Arunachal Pradesh during the period when it was under NEFA. Arunachal Pradesh was declared Union Territory (UT) in 1972 and with the formation of Union Territory, educational development got accelerated. All the schools were affiliated to Central Board of Secondary Education (CBSE), New Delhi, and English was adopted as the medium of instruction. Government of Arunachal Pradesh took interest in the educational development of the state and as a result, large numbers of schools were opened in the state.

Table 3.1: Type of Schools till 2004-05

Schools	Govt. of Arunachal Pradesh	Private & Other	Total
Higher Secondary	60	18	78
Secondary	94	42	136
Secondary level of School	154(8.37)	60(22.99)	214(10.18)
Upper Primary	438	57	495
Primary	11249	122	1371
Pre-Primary	0	22	22
Elementary	1687	201	1888
	1841	261	2102

Source: Office of the Director of School Education, Government of Arunachal Pradesh, Itanagar.

Secondary Education in Arunachal Pradesh followed the primary and middle levels of Education after Independence. The beginning of formal primary education dates back to early twentieth century, and even to nineteenth century, the efforts towards formalizing education in schools did not sustain for long due to which not much effort was made towards introducing Secondary Education in the state before Independence. The first high school of the state was established at Pasighat during the academic session 1951-52. Later two more high schools were established at Along and Tezu during the first Five Year Plan which started functioning much later during 1947-48. The secondary schools which were established during first Five Year Plan started functioning from the following plan period when there were eligible students from 15 middle schools established by 1955-56. Thus, the need for secondary schools was a compelling factor to upgrade two middle schools to secondary schools during the second Five Year Plan.

The history of the growth of Secondary Education also suffers from data inconsistency probably because of improper classification and a lack of proper maintenance of records in the education department, and another reason more probably could be damage of records when the departments were shifted from Shillong to Itanagar in early 1970s and the subsequent bifurcation and reorganization of the education department. However, census surveys and available earlier writings help us to formulate the history of evolution of Secondary Education in the state.

At the beginning, all the schools were government schools and they were located in the district headquarters. At that time, secondary schools were established at Khonsa, Tezu, Pasighat, Along, Ziro, Bomdila, Doimukh, Itanagar, Seppa, and Tawang. In other words, secondary level schools were established at the administrative headquarters having potential to grow rapidly into urban centre. However, most of the schools in secondary level came into existence between early 1980s and 1990s because of political consideration in upgrading middle and secondary schools. As a result, secondary schools were established in rural and inaccessible areas like Nyapin, Palin, Mechuka, Tuting, Chayangtajo, Sagalee, Rumgong, etc. during that period. In the year 2002, only 156 secondary level schools were recorded in the rural areas of the state.

Table 3.2: Growth of Higher Secondary and Secondary Education Over the Years from 1971 to 2004-05

Particulars	Government & Private	Higher Secondary			Secondary			Total		
		1971	1999-2000	2004-2005	1971	1999-2000	2004-2005	1971	1999-2000	2004-2005
School	Government	09	55	60	11	88	94	20	143	154
	Private and other	-	13	18	-	20	42	-	33	60
	Total	09	68	78	11	108	136	20	176	214
Teacher	Government	146	1420	1894	147	1292	1662	293	2612	3556
	Private and other	-	374	NA	-	372	NA	-	746	
	Total	146	1794	1894	147	1664	1662	293	3458	3556
Enrolment	Government	71	-	14176	147		27343	-	-	41519
	Private and other	-	-	-						-
	Total	71	-	14176	147		27343			41519

Source: Office of the Director of School Education, Itanagar.

Interpretation: The above table reveals the growth of both Higher Secondary and Secondary Education from 1971 to 2005, taking into consideration the total number of schools, teachers, and students' enrolment. It is evident from the history of education in Arunachal Pradesh that there is a growth of both levels of schools in the state. There were only 9 government higher secondary schools during 1971 which rose to 55 and 60 during the academic sessions 1999-2000 and 2004-05 respectively. Likewise, the private and other higher secondary schools have risen from 0 in 1971 to 13 and 18 during the academic sessions 1999-2000 and 2004-05 respectively. The total number of schools both government and private at higher secondary level were 09 in 1971, 68 during 1999-2000, and 78 during 2004-05. Similarly, from 11 government secondary schools in 1971, the number rose to 88 and 94 during the academic sessions 1999-2000 and 2004-05 respectively. Likewise, the private and other secondary level schools rose from 0 in 1971 to 20 and 42 during the academic sessions 1999-2000 and 2004-05 respectively. The total number of schools both government and private at secondary level were 11 in 1971, 108 during 1999-2000, and 136 during 2004-05.

The overall schools, both government and private and both secondary and higher secondary levels were 20 in 1971, 176 during 1999-2000, and 214 during 2004-05 in the state.

There were 146 government higher secondary school teachers in 1971 which rose to 1420 during 1999-2000 and 1894 during 2004-05. In the private higher secondary schools, there were 374 teachers during 1999-2000. On the other hand, at the secondary level, there were 147 teachers in the government schools in 1971 which rose to 1292 during 1999-2000 and 1662 during 2004-05. The private secondary schools had 372 teachers during 1999-2000. The overall teachers, both government and private and at both secondary and higher secondary levels were 293 in 1971, 3458 during 1999-2000, and 3556 during 2004-05 in the state.

Based on the availability of the sources, it came to light that in 1971, there were 71 enrolments of students in the government higher secondary schools of Arunachal Pradesh which rose to 14176 during the session 2004-05. Similarly, in the secondary schools, there were 147 enrolments of students in 1971 and 27343 during the session 2004-05. The overall students' enrolment in the state was 41519.

Table 3.3: Growth of Secondary Education in Arunachal Pradesh Over the Years

Category	Management	2013	2014	2015	2016	2017	2018	Overall Total
Schools	Govt.	215	211	243	264	282	285	1500
	Private	71	75	84	89	104	109	532
Teachers	Govt.	3979	3662	4505	4630	4898	5860	27534
	Private	1003	1218	1371	1513	1681	1743	8529
Enrolment	Govt.	18096	13577	18639	19098	19131	18063	106604
	Private	2036	2177	2379	2714	2563	2698	14567

Source: U-DISE (Unified District Information System for Education)

Interpretation: The above table indicates the growth of Secondary Education in Arunachal Pradesh over the years in terms of schools, teachers, and enrolment of students. From the above table, it can be observed that there has been growth of secondary schools in both government and private sectors in the state. In the year 2013, there were 215 government and 71 private schools which rose to 285 government and 109 private schools at the secondary level in the year 2018. However, in 2014, the government secondary schools had reduced to 211 from 215. Apart from this, in every year both government and private schools have been increasing year after year.

In the year 2013, there were 3979 government and 1003 private secondary school teachers which rose to 5860 government and 1743 private secondary school teachers in the year 2018. In the government secondary schools, the number of teachers has been increasing year after year expect in the year 2014, whereas in private secondary schools, the number of teachers has been increasing every year starting from 2013.

Unlike the increasing numbers of schools and teachers, the U-DISE source reveals that the students' enrolment particularly of 10th grade at the secondary schools has not been increasing year by year as in government schools, 18096 students had enrolled in 2013 and in 2018, the number of students' enrolment was only 18063. The maximum number of students enrolled in the secondary schools was in the year 2017 in case of government schools. In the private schools, the year 2016 had witnessed the maximum number of students' enrolment in the secondary schools which was followed by the year 2018 and then 2017.

Table 3.4: Status of Teachers (2004-05)

Type of School	No. of Trained Teachers	No. of Untrained Teachers	Total No. of Teachers
Higher Secondary	1242	652	1894
Secondary	815	847	1662
Total	2057 (57.85%)	1499 (42.15%)	3556

Source: Office of the Director of School Education, Government of Arunachal Pradesh.

Interpretation: The above table indicates the status of teachers in terms of trained and untrained during the academic session 2004-05. In the higher secondary schools, there were 1242 trained and 652 untrained teachers during the academic session 2004-05. Combining both trained and untrained teachers, there were total 1894 higher secondary school teachers. In the secondary schools, there were 815 trained and 847 untrained teachers. Combining both trained and untrained teachers, there were total 1662 secondary school teachers in the state.

The comparative data are not available to present the growth of number of teachers in secondary level schools over the years. However, it gives an idea of the status of teachers in the secondary level schools. Out of the overall total of teachers in both secondary and higher secondary schools, i.e., 3556 teachers, 2057 (57.85%) teachers were trained and 1499 (42.15%) teachers were untrained.

Table 3.5: District-Wise Teacher Details (2018-19)

District	Total School	Total Teacher	Gender		Academic			Professional		
			Male	Female	UG	G	PG	B. Ed	M. Ed	Others
Tawang	131	866	461	405	137	502	227	219	7	50
West Kameng	219	1351	649	702	310	678	363	355	20	129
East Kameng	262	1231	788	443	308	627	296	269	14	53
Papumpare	434	3567	1533	2034	872	1824	871	975	31	196
L/Subansiri	217	1398	711	687	277	785	336	436	18	101
Upper Subansiri	232	1108	705	403	321	648	139	167	6	82
W/Siang	191	1370	754	616	224	805	341	556	5	198
East Siang	165	1791	930	861	251	1103	437	773	26	141
U/Siang	131	759	517	242	207	375	177	223	17	41
Dibang Valley	25	153	81	72	40	86	27	37	3	3
Lohit	106	723	348	375	139	407	177	204	6	1
Changlang	344	1723	979	744	401	970	352	431	14	107
Tirap	150	809	399	410	229	414	166	163	19	73
Kurung Kumey	185	700	432	268	266	342	92	175	5	46
L/Dibang Valley	99	885	440	445	164	475	246	316	7	39
Anjaw	85	358	244	114	109	175	74	85	3	17
Longding	105	549	267	282	182	263	104	160	10	50
Namsai	223	1254	646	608	306	710	238	309	9	202
Kra-Daadi	123	767	465	302	337	318	112	156	2	13
Siang	140	727	459	268	161	374	192	186	4	13
Lower Siang	138	884	581	303	194	443	247	292	20	113
Kamle	88	412	275	137	150	181	81	90	7	27
Total	3793	23385	12664	10721	5585	12505	5295	6577	253	1695

Source: U-DISE (Unified District Information System for Education)

Interpretation: The above table displays the details of teachers teaching in various districts of Arunachal Pradesh. In 2018-19, there were 23385 teachers teaching in 3793 schools of the state. Papum Pare had the highest number of teachers, i.e., 3567, compared to all other districts of Arunachal Pradesh whereas, the lowest number of teachers was found in Dibang Valley district with only 153 teachers. Not surprisingly, Papum Pare has the highest number of schools (434) and the district of Dibang Valley has the lowest number of schools (25). The district of Anjaw comes next to Dibang Valley in terms of having lowest schools (85) and teachers (358). Thus, the number of teachers are in proportion to the number of schools present in these districts. However, it is not the case for all the other districts. The number of teachers are not in proportion to the schools present in various other districts. For example, Changlang is second to Papum Pare in terms of number of schools with 344 schools and 1723 teachers whereas, East Siang follows Papum Pare in terms of having highest number of teachers (1791). It means that the number of schools and the number of teachers are not necessarily in proportion.

From the above table, it is clear that male teachers were more than the female teachers in the schools of Arunachal Pradesh. There were 12664 male teachers compared to 10721 female teachers in the year 2018-19. Considering the academic status, 5585 teachers were Under Graduate, 12505 teachers were Graduate, and 5295 teachers were Post Graduate. Interestingly, the highest number of Under Graduate teachers (872), Graduate teachers (1,824), and Post Graduate teachers (871) were found in the district of Papum Pare and the lowest number of Under Graduate teachers (40), Graduate teachers (86), and Post Graduate teachers (27) were found in the district of Dibang Valley.

With respect to professional degree, the highest number of teachers with B.Ed. degree were in Papum Pare district (975 teachers), followed by East Siang (773 teachers) and West Siang (556 teachers). Whereas, the lowest number of teachers with B.Ed. degree were in Dibang Valley (37 teachers), followed by Anjaw (85 teachers) and Kamle (90 teachers). Teachers with M.Ed. degree were highest in Papum Pare (31 teachers), followed by East Siang (26 teachers) and both Lower Siang

(20 teachers) and West Kameng (20 teachers). On the other hand, the lowest number of teachers holding M.Ed. degree were in the district of Kra-Daadi with only two teachers holding M.Ed. degree, followed by Anjaw and Dibang Valley with only three M.Ed. holder teachers each. Apart from this, some of the teachers were trained with some other degrees. There were 1695 teachers with professional degrees other than B.Ed. and M.Ed. Combining all the selected districts, there were 6577 teachers with B.Ed. degree and only 253 teachers with M.Ed. degree. Thereby, the maximum number of teachers were trained with B.Ed. degree. In proportion to the total population of teachers and total number of schools, Papum Pare had the highest number of trained teachers (1202) and Dibang Valley had the lowest number of trained teachers (43). Altogether, the total number of trained teachers in Arunachal Pradesh were 8525, indicating that many teachers were still untrained.

Objective II: *To investigate the Enrolment, Promotion, Repetition, and Dropout rates of Students at the Secondary Stage of Selected Districts.*

Here we shall first consider the enrolment of students in the secondary schools of the selected districts. Then we shall proceed to study the promotion, repetition, and dropout rates of students at the secondary stage of the selected districts.

(a) ***Enrolment of Students in the Government Secondary Schools.***

Table 3.6: Enrolment of Students at the Secondary Stage of the Selected Districts.

Stage	Gender	2013	2014	2015	2016	2017	Total
Secondary Stage (Particularly 10th Grade)	Boys	9292	7052	9398	9626	9501	44869
	Girls	8804	6525	9241	9472	9630	43672
Total		18096	13577	18639	19098	19131	88541
Higher Secondary (Particularly 10+2)	Boys	6807	3731	6507	6725	6782	30552
	Girls	5863	3482	6285	6557	6806	28993
Total		12670	7213	12792	13282	13588	59545

Source: U-DISE (Unified District Information System for Education)

Interpretation: Starting from the year 2013, there has been an increasing rate of enrolment among the 10th grade secondary school students except for the year 2014 when the total enrolments of boys and girls taken together was 13577. During the academic sessions from 2013 to 2016, the enrolments of boys in the secondary schools at 10th grade were 9292, 7052, 9398, and 9626 respectively whereas, the enrolments of girls were 8804, 6525, 9241, and 9472 respectively. This explains that in all these years, the enrolments of boys were higher than that of the girls. But, in the academic year 2017, the enrolments among boys were 9501 and among girls, it was 9630, which revealed that the enrolments among girls were higher than that of boys at 10th grade in the government secondary schools. Altogether, there were 88,541 students' enrolments in the secondary schools at 10th grade during 2013-2017.

Starting from the year 2013, there has been an increasing rate of enrolment among the higher secondary school students except for the year 2014 when the total enrolments of boys and girls taken together was 7213. During the academic sessions from 2013 to 2016, the enrolments of boys in the higher secondary schools were 6807, 3731, 6507, and 6725 respectively, whereas the enrolments among girls were 5863, 3482, 6285, and 6557 respectively. In all these years, the enrolments of boys were higher than that of the girls. But, in the academic year 2017, the enrolments among boys were 6782 and among girls, it was 6806, which revealed that the enrolments among girls were higher than that of boys at the higher secondary level in the government higher secondary schools. Altogether, there were 59545 students' enrolments in the higher secondary schools at 10+2 grade during 2013-2017.

Thus, we find that in every year from 2013 to 2017, the enrolments of students at 10th grade were higher than that of 10+2 grade students in the government schools of Arunachal Pradesh.

(b) *Promotion, Repetition, and Dropout Rates of Secondary School Students in the Government Schools.*

Table 3.7: Promotion, Repetition, and Dropout Rates of Students at the Secondary Stage of the Selected Districts.

Stage	Repetition, Promotion and Dropout rates of Sec. School Students from 2013-2017														
10th Grade Students	2013			2014			2015			2016			2017		
	RR %	PR %	DR %	RR %	PR %	DR %	RR %	PR %	DR %	RR %	PR %	DR %	RR %	PR %	DR %
	3.75 %	11.75 %	0.0 %	2.16 %	49.95 %	0.0 %	1.10 %	71.76 %	0.0 %	0.70 %%	82.44 %	0.0 %	0.73 %	42.98 %	0.0 %

RR = Repetition Rate, PR = Promotion Rate, and DR = Dropout Rate

Source: U-DISE (Unified District Information System for Education)

Interpretation: Since the implementation of Continuous and Comprehensive Evaluation (CCE) pattern of evaluation, the dropout rate of the students at the secondary school stage, particularly of the 10th grade students, has dropped down to 0% in all the districts of Arunachal Pradesh. Likewise, the above table shows 0% dropout rate in all the selected districts of Arunachal Pradesh during the academic sessions from 2013 to 2016. Fortunately, after the removal of CCE pattern of evaluation in 2017, it is seen that there is still 0% dropout rate in the districts of Arunachal Pradesh.

Apart from the 0% dropout rate of the secondary school students in Arunachal Pradesh, it is observed that the repetition rate of secondary school students were 3.75%, 2.16%, 1.10%, 0.70%, and 0.73% for the academic sessions 2013, 2014, 2015, 2016, and 2017, respectively. Although there is no example of dropout, there has been repetition in the secondary schools of the state. As far as promotion rate is concerned, the state had 11.75% promotion rate of secondary school students in the year 2013, 49.95% in 2014, 71.76% in 2015, 82.44% in 2016, and 42.98% in the year 2017.

It can be observed that there is a strong relationship among repetition, dropout, and poor performance of the students. A school that expects good performance from its students should follow up the dropout rate of the students along with the repetition rate and put efforts to solve such problems.

Objective III: *To Explore the Administrative Set up for the Functioning of Secondary Education.*

The state of Arunachal Pradesh has been divided administratively into districts, a district into sub-division/Extra Assistant Commissioner (EAC) headquarters and these further into circles. In the same way, the administration pertaining to education has also been organized at the state and district levels and down below at sub-division or circles. Presently, at state level, the organizational structure includes a Ministry, a Secretariat, and Directorates. The functions of these three bodies include policy formulation, implementation, monitoring, and supervision.

At district level, there is Deputy Director of School Education (DDSE) who functions as an implementation, monitoring, and supervision body. Below district level, there is Assistant District Education Officer (ADEO)/Adult Education Supervisor (AES) attached to either EAC Officer or CO office when there is less number of schools. Since, ADEOs/AESs mainly supervise the schools, the secondary school activities are taken up by the DDSE and then by the District Project Coordinators (DPCs) followed by Block Resource Centres (BRCs), Cluster Resource Centres (CRCs), and the concerned head of various secondary schools.

The Government of Arunachal Pradesh has bifurcated the Directorate of School Education into two directorates on 28th October 2010. They are Directorate of Elementary Education and Directorate of Secondary Education. But, no proper bifurcation of the directorates has been taken so far although they are functioning separately for the last two years. Therefore, proper bifurcation is important for stream lining and smooth functioning of the two directorates. Earlier, DPCs had two separate administrative functions for elementary and secondary schools but now both are integrated into one post after the implementation of Samagra Shiksha. It is to be observed that there is no change in the administrative functions of the Secondary Education system except that the composite budget fund has been changed in the state with the merging of centrally sponsored scheme of SSA, RMSA, and Teacher Education (TE). Accordingly, the scheme has been developed and launched to form an Integrated Scheme on School Education/Samagra Shiksha from pre-schools to secondary schools.

Objective IV: *To Investigate the Availability of Infrastructure Facilities in Secondary Schools.*

In order to investigate the availability of infrastructure facilities, three groups of sample were drawn from the population in the present study such as Principals/Headmasters, Teachers, and the Students of the secondary schools in Arunachal Pradesh. First of all, the responses made by the Government and Private Secondary School Headmasters/Principals on infrastructure facilities were separately explained after which, the responses of teachers and the students were presented in the same manner by separating the responses of government and private management.

Table 3.8: Responses of the Government and Private Secondary School Headmasters/Principals Regarding Infrastructure Facilities

Sl. No.	Items/ Questions	Response	Govt. %	Private %
1.	Does the school have own land?	Yes	100%	95%
		No	0%	5%
2.	Does the school have own school building?	Yes	100%	95%
		No	0%	5%
3.	What type of school building do you have?	a) Permanent b) Rented	95% 5%	90% 10%
4.	What is the structure of your school building?	a) Assam type b) RCC type c) Kachha	55% 45 % 0%	5%
5.	Does your school have sufficient playground?	Yes	35%	80%
		No	65%	65%

Sl. No.	Items/ Questions	Response	Govt. %	Private %
6.	Does your school have boundary wall?	Yes	45%	35%
		No	55%	65%
7.	Does your school have motor able road connection?	Yes	75%	35%
		No	25%	90%
8.	Do you have hostel facility for the students in your school?	Yes	55%	10%
		No	45%	85%
9.	Does your school have sufficient furniture?	Yes	45%	15%
		No	55%	85%
10.	Does your school have Ramp/Railing facility for the physically challenged?	Yes	25%	15%
		No	75%	5%
11.	Does your school provide First-Aid facilities for the students?	Yes	35%	85%
		No	65%	15%
12.	Is there any provision for separate toilet rooms for both boys and girls?	Yes	45%	90%
		No	55%	10%
13.	Do you get adequate/ safe drinking water supply in your school?	Yes	30%	75%
		No	70%	25%

Sl. No.	Items/ Questions	Response	Govt. %	Private %
14.	Do you have school library?	Yes	35%	65%
		No	65%	35%
15.	What are the facilities you have in the library?	a) Adequate books	20%	65%
		b) Equipped furniture	10%	60%
		c) Journals	5%	55%
		d) Encylopedia	10%	60%
16.	What types of Audio-Visual Aids are provided in your school?	a) LCD projectors	55%	45%
		b) Tape recorder	0%	10%
		c) Computer lab	35%	50%
		d) OHP	5%	20%
17.	Do you have school laboratory for Science students?	Yes	20%	75%
		No	80%	25%
18.	What are the facilities you have in the Laboratory?	a) Laboratory room	60%	75%
		b) Apparatus & equipments	25%	60%
		c) Proper furniture	20%	40%
19.	Select the following facilities available in your school.	a) Auditorium	40%	50%
		b) Teachers' Quarter	55%	80%
		c) Principal's office	75%	90%
		d) Staff's room	90%	85%
		e) EDUSAT/Internet connection	35%	45%
		f) Computer room	50%	70%
		g) Smart classroom	60%	40%
		h) Store room	65%	85%

Sl. No.	Items/ Questions	Response		Govt. %		Private %	
20.	What are the physical conditions of your school classroom? (a) Desk and Benches (Sufficient/ Insufficient), (b) Blackboard (Good in condition/Bad in condition), (c) Fans (In order/Out of order), (d) Electricity (Available/Not Available) and (e) Properly ventilated (Yes/No)	a) Sufficient	Insufficient	55 %	45%	85%	15%
		b) Good in condition	Bad in condition	65%	35%	85%	15%
		c) In order	Out of order	60%	40%	65%	35%
		d) Available	Not available	60%	40%	95%	5%
		e) Yes	No	75%	25%	95%	5%

Interpretation: The above table reveals the responses of the government and private secondary school headmasters/ principals regarding infrastructure facilities. It indicates that:

- 100% of Government Secondary Schools have their own land while 5% Private Secondary Schools do not have their own land.
- 100% of Government Secondary Schools operate from their own buildings whereas 5% Private Secondary Schools operate from rented school buildings.
- 95% of Government Secondary Schools operate from permanent school buildings and 5% from temporary buildings whereas 90% Private Secondary Schools operate from permanent school buildings and 10% from temporary buildings.
- 55% of Government Secondary School buildings are of Assamese type and 45% of RCC type whereas

only 5% of Private Secondary School buildings are of Assamese type.

- 35% of Government Secondary Schools have sufficient playground whereas in case of Private Schools it is 80%.
- 45% of Government Secondary Schools have boundary wall whereas in case of Private Schools it is 35%.
- 75% of Government Secondary Schools are connected with motorable roads whereas only 35% of Private Schools have this facility.
- 55% of Government Secondary Schools have hostel facility for the students in their schools whereas only 10% of Private Schools have this facility.
- 45% of Government Secondary Schools have sufficient furniture whereas in case of Private Schools it is 15%.
- 25% of Government Secondary Schools have ramp/ railing facility for the physically challenged whereas only 15% of Private Schools have this facility.
- 35% of Government Secondary Schools have First-Aid facilities for the students whereas 85% of Private Schools have this facility.
- 45% of Government Secondary Schools have separate toilet rooms for both boys and girls whereas in case of Private Schools it is 90%.
- 30% of Government Secondary Schools have adequate/ save drinking water supply whereas 75% of Private Schools have this facility.
- 35% of Government Secondary Schools have school library whereas in case of Private Schools it is 65%.
- 20% of Government Secondary Schools have libraries with adequate books, 10% equipped with furniture, 5% have journals, and 10% have Encyclopedia whereas 65% of the Private Schools' libraries have adequate books, 60% equipped with furniture, 55% have journals, and 60% have Encyclopedia in their shelves.

- 55% of Government Secondary Schools have LCD projectors, 35% have computer labs, and 5% have over head projectors (OHP) whereas in case of Private Schools, 45% have LCD projectors, 10% have tape recorders, 50% have computer labs, and 20% have OHPs.
- 20% of Government Secondary Schools have laboratories for science students whereas 75% of Private Schools have this facility.
- 60% of Government Secondary Schools have laboratory rooms, 25% have apparatus and equipments, and 20% have proper furniture whereas 75% of Private Schools have laboratory rooms, 60% have apparatus and equipments, and 40% have proper furniture.
- 95% of Government Secondary Schools have auditoriums, 55% quarters for teachers, 75% Principals' offices, 90% staff's rooms, 35% EDUSAT/internet connections, 50% computer rooms, 60% smart classrooms, and 65% store rooms whereas 50% Private Schools have auditoriums, 80% quarters for teachers, 90% Principals' offices, 85% staff's rooms, 45% EDUSAT/internet connections, 70% computer rooms, 40% smart classrooms, and 85% store rooms.
- 55% of Government Secondary Schools have sufficient desks and benches, 65% blackboards in good condition, 60% running fans, 60% with electricity, and 75% with proper ventilations whereas 85% of Private Schools have sufficient desks and benches, 85% blackboards in good condition, 65% running fans, 95% with electricity, and 95% with proper ventilations.

Table 3.9: Responses of Government and Private Secondary School Teachers Regarding Infrastructure Facilities.

Sl. No.	Items/Questions	Response	Govt. %	Pvt. %
1.	Do you have sufficient infrastructure in your staff room?	Yes	57.68%	82.59%
		No	42.31%	17.40%

Sl. No.	Items/Questions	Response	Govt. %	Pvt. %
2.	Does your school provide Laboratory facilities for science students?	Yes	22.88%	72.59%
		No	77.11%	27.40%
3.	Do you face problem in using Audio-Visual aids/ Teaching aids in the classroom?	Yes	32.91%	10.74%
		No	67.08%	89.25%
4.	Do you face any problem in the School Library?	Yes	51.72%	10.37%
		No	48.27%	89.62%
5.	Do you get adequate drinking water facility?	Yes	35.42%	84.81%
		No	64.57%	15.18%
6.	Are there separate toilet rooms for male and female teachers?	Yes	67.39%	82.22%
		No	32.60%	17.77%
7.	Do you get transportation facilities?	Yes	5.01%	63.33%
		No	94.98%	36.66%

Interpretation: The above table reveals the responses of the government and private secondary school teachers regarding infrastructure facilities. It indicates that:

- 57.65% of Government Secondary School Teachers accepted that there is sufficient infrastructure in the staff rooms whereas in case of Private Secondary School Teachers it is 82.59%.
- 22.88% of Government Secondary School Teachers accepted to provide laboratory facilities for science students whereas in case of Private Secondary School Teachers it is 72.59%.
- 32.91% of Government Secondary School Teachers face problems in using Audio-Visual Aids/Teaching Aids in the classrooms whereas in case of Private Secondary School Teachers it is only 10.74%.
- 51.72% of Government Secondary School Teachers faces problems in the school library whereas in case of Private Secondary School Teachers it is only 10.37%.

- 35.42% of Government Secondary School Teachers believe that there is adequate drinking water facility in the schools whereas for Private Secondary School Teachers it is 84.81%.
- 67.39% of Government Secondary School Teachers accepted to have separate toilet rooms for male and female teachers whereas in case of Private Secondary School Teachers it is 82.22%.
- 5.01% of Government Secondary School Teachers accepted to get transportation facilities from schools whereas in case of Private Secondary School Teachers it is 63.33%.

Table 3.10: Responses of Government and Private Secondary School Students Regarding Infrastructure Facilities.

Sl. No.	Items/ Questions	Response		Govt. %		Pvt. %	
1.	What are the physical conditions of your school classroom? (a) Desk and Benches (Sufficient/ Insufficient), (b) Blackboard (Good in condition/Bad in condition), (c) Fans (In order/Out of order), (d) Electricity (Available/Not Available) and (e) Properly ventilated (Yes/No)	(a) Sufficient	Insufficient	30.25%	67.74%	88.73%	11.26%
		(b) Good in Condition	Bad in condition	29.34%	70.65%	84.02%	15.97%
		(c) In order	Out of order	38.08%	61.91%	67.01%	32.98%
		(d) Available	Not available	45.67%	54.32%	58.04%	41.95%
		(e) Yes	No	52.01%	47.98%	81.83%	18.16%

2.	Do you have the following facilities in your school?	(a) Auditorium Hall	31.65%	63.21%
		(b) Playground	67.02%	80.22%
		(c) Hostel Facility	28.93%	74.48%
		(d) Career Counseling Cell	7.41%	5.74%
		(e) EDUSAT/Internet connection	6.59%	9.08%
		(f) Computer Room	31.98%	67.24%
		(g) Smart classroom	43.52%	27.01%
3.	Do you have laboratory facility in your school?	Yes	23.82%	54.94%
		No	76.17%	45.05%
4.	Do you have school library?	Yes	17.39%	88.16%
		No	82.60%	11.83%
5.	Do you get adequate safe drinking water facility?	Yes	18.30%	45.86%
		No	81.69%	54.13%
6.	Are there separate toilets for boys and girls?	Yes	38.41%	97.58%
		No	61.58%	2.41%
7.	Do you have bus transportation service in your school?	Yes	3.70%	63.67%
		No	96.29%	36.32%

Interpretation: The above table reveals the responses of the government and private secondary school students regarding infrastructure facilities. It indicates that:

- 30.25% of Government Secondary School Students accepted to have sufficient desks and benches in their schools whereas in case of Private Secondary School Students it is 88.73%.
- 29.34% of Government Secondary School Students accepted to have good condition blackboards in their schools whereas in case of Private Secondary School Students it is 84.02%.
- 38.08% of Government Secondary School Students accepted to have good condition fans in their schools

whereas in case of Private Secondary School Students it is 67.01%.

- 45.67% of Government Secondary School Students accepted to have electricity in their schools whereas in case of Private Secondary School Students it is 58.04%.
- 52.01% of Government Secondary School Students accepted to have properly ventilated class rooms whereas in case of Private Secondary School Students it is 81.83%.
- 31.65% of Government Secondary School Students accepted to have auditorium halls, 67.02% playgrounds, 28.93% hostel facilities, 7.41% career counselling cells, 6.59% EDUSAT/internet connections, 31.98% computer rooms, and 43.52% smart classrooms in their schools whereas 63.21% Private Secondary School Students accepted to have auditorium halls, 80.22% playgrounds, 74.48% hostel facilities, 5.74% career counselling cells, 9.08% EDUSAT/internet connections, 67.24% computer rooms, and 27.01% smart classrooms in their schools.
- 23.82% of Government Secondary School Students accepted to have laboratory facilities in their schools whereas in case of Private Secondary School Students it is 54.94%.
- 17.39% of Government Secondary School Students accepted to have libraries in their schools whereas in case of Private Secondary School Students it is 88.16.
- 18.30% of Government Secondary School Students accepted to have adequate safe drinking water facilities in their schools whereas in case of Private Secondary School Students it is 45.86%.
- 38.41% of Government Secondary School Students accepted to have separate toilets for boys and girls in their school whereas in case of Private Secondary School Students it is 97.58%.

- 3.7% of Government Secondary School Students accepted to have bus transportation services in their schools whereas in case of Private Secondary School Students it is 63.67%.

Objective V: *To examine the academic achievement of Secondary School Students of Arunachal Pradesh.*

This objective aims at examining the academic achievement of secondary school students of Arunachal Pradesh. Based on the objective, one hypothesis was framed—there exists no significant difference between the academic achievements of 10th grade students in Arunachal Pradesh before and after the removal of Continuous and Comprehensive Evaluation (CCE) pattern.

Before testing the significant difference, academic achievement of secondary school students, particularly 10th grade students, were computed by showing the district-wise comparison of academic achievement of both government and the private secondary schools students of the state. Further, the year-wise trend analyses on the academic achievements of the 10th grade students from the academic sessions 2013-2018 were also done.

Table 3.11: District-wise Comparison of Academic Achievement of the 10th Grade Students of the Government Secondary Schools.

Sl. No.	District	2012-13	2013-14	2014-15	2015-16	2016-17	2017-18	Average %
1.	Anjaw	74.44%	91%	75.90%	73%	38%	71.49%	70.63%
2.	Changlang	68.52%	89%	91%	81%	54%	84.25%	77.96%
3.	Dibang Valley	43.39%	76.23%	81%	92%	83%	96.66%	78.71%
4.	East Kameng	92.52%	92.16%	69%	77%	96%	88.26%	85.82%
5.	East Siang	80%	87%	79%	80%	53%	86.66%	77.61%
6.	Kra-daadi					31%	40.16%	35.58%
7.	Kurung Kumey	68.08%	96.07%	88%	54%	39%	63.59%	68.12%
8.	Lohit	70.90%	76%	86%	75%	56%	56.04%	69.99%
9.	Longding					78%	88.83%	83.41%

Sl. No.	District	2012-13	2013-14	2014-15	2015-16	2016-17	2017-18	Average %
10.	Lower Dibang Valley	39.91%	77%	69%	79%	72%	91.38%	71.38%
11.	Lower Subansiri	64.08%	75.01%	81%	71%	69%	90.58%	75.11%
12.	Namsai					50%	78.38%	64.19%
13.	Papumpare	76.20%	82%	81%	66%	60%	65.38%	71.76%
14.	Siang					56%	-	56%
15.	Tawang	98.25%	93.24%	100%	81%	84%	98.19%	92.44%
16.	Tirap	79.17%	77%	61%	44%	58%	70.65%	64.97%
17.	Upper Siang	82.83%	61%	60%	57%	52%	91.42%	67.37%
18.	Upper Subansiri	92.91%	88.63%	60%	36%	69%	74.35%	70.14%
19.	West Kameng	73.20%	81.42%	88%	67%	43%	87.09%	73.28%
20.	West Siang	87.71%	89.39%	88%	59.50%	63%	43.80%	71.9%

Source: U-DISE (Unified District Information System for Education)

Interpretation: The above table shows the district-wise academic performance of the 10th grade government secondary school students during the academic sessions 2013 to 2018. Besides, the average percentage of the academic achievement of the students has been shown in the extreme right column of the table. The data in the table depicts the pass percentage of the 10th grade students in yearly order. Among the 20 selected districts, Tawang has the highest average pass percentage of 92.44% among the 10th grade students. It is followed by East Kameng with the average pass percentage of 85.82% and Longding with 83.41%. On the other hand, the lowest average pass percentage is seen in the district of Kra-Daadi with the average pass percentage of 35.58% in the two academic years. In the most districts, the average pass percentage of the 10th grade students falls within the range of 70% to 80%—Anjaw (70.63%), Changlang (77.96%), Dibang Valley (78.71%), East Siang (77.61%), Lower Dibang Valley (71.38%), Lower Subansiri (75.11%), Papum Pare (71.76%), Upper Subansiri (70.14%), West Kameng (73.28%), and West Siang (71.9%). In rest of the selected districts, the average pass percentage of 10th grade students lies between 50% to 70%.

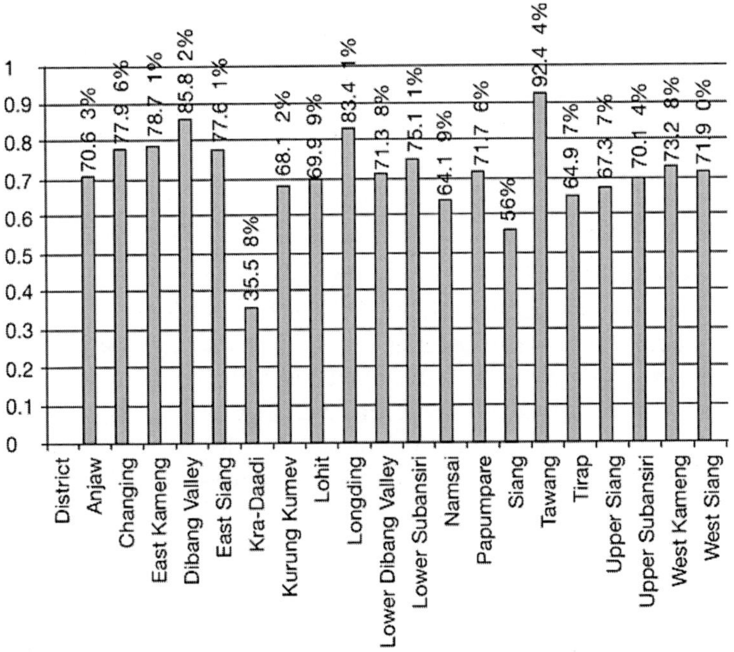

Figure 3.1: District-wise Comparison of Academic Achievement of the 10th Grade Students of Government Secondary Schools.

Table 3.12: District-wise Comparison of Academic Achievement of the 10th Grade Students of Private Secondary Schools.

Sl. No.	District	2012-13	2013-14	2014-15	2015-16	2016-17	Average %
1.	Anjaw	100%	100%	-	100%	97%	99.25%
2.	Changlang	97.95%	94%	100%	97%	96%	96.99%
3.	Dibang Valley	100%	100%	-	100%	93%	98.25%
4.	East Kameng	100%	100%	100%	98%	99%	99.4%
5.	East Siang	99.42%	100%	100%	93.66%	94%	97.41%
6.	Kurung Kumey	96.55%	100%	100%	98%	98.57%	98.62%
7.	Lohit	98.63%	100%	-	95%	97%	97.65%
8.	Lower Dibang Valley	100%		100%	94.25%	25%	79.81%
9.	Lower Subansiri	99.14%	100%	99.45%	98.57%	99%	99.23%
10.	Papumpare	98.36%	99.30%	95.61%	99%	98%	98.05%
11.	Tawang	97.22%	98%	100%	100%	98%	98.64%
12.	Tirap	98.79%	99%	77.55%	100%	98%	94.66%

Sl. No.	District	2012-13	2013-14	2014-15	2015-16	2016-17	Average %
13.	Upper Siang	97.5%	100%	100%	100%	97.24%	98.94%
14.	Upper Subansiri	98%	100%	100%	99.66%	99.44%	99.42%
15.	West Kameng	100%	100%	100%	100%	98%	99.6%
16.	West Siang	89.77%	93%	92.77%	92.3%	98%	93.16

Source: U-DISE (Unified District Information System for Education)

Interpretation: The above table shows the district-wise academic performance of the 10th grade students of private secondary schools of Arunachal Pradesh during the sessions 2013 to 2017. Besides, the average percentage of the academic achievement of the students has been shown in the extreme right column of the table. Among the 20 selected districts, West Kameng has the highest average pass percentage of 99.6% among the 10th grade students. It is followed by Upper Subansiri with the average pass percentage of 99.42% and East Kameng with

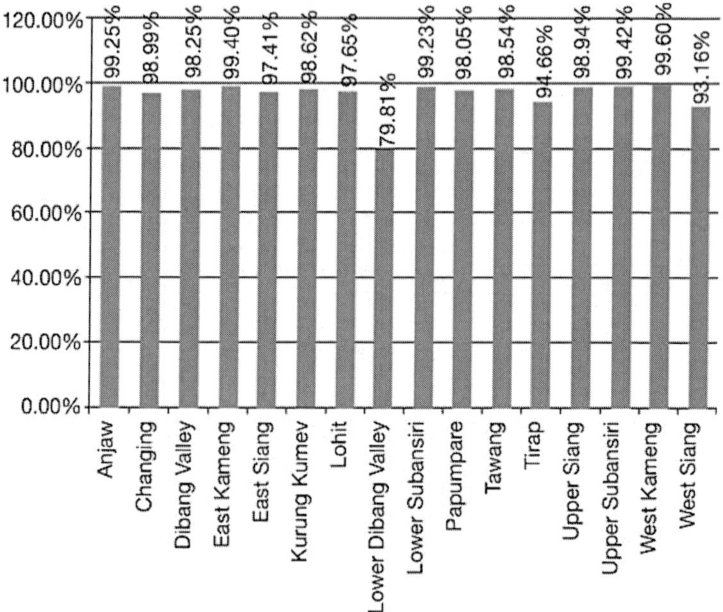

Figure 3.2: District-wise Comparison of Academic Achievement of the 10th Grade Students of Private Secondary Schools.

99.4%. On the other hand, Lower Dibang Valley has the lowest average pass percentage of 79.81%. In the most districts, the average pass percentage of the 10th grade students falls above 90%—Anjaw (99.25%), Changlang (96.99%), Dibang Valley (98.25%), East Siang (97.41%), Kurung Kumey (98.62%), Lohit (97.65%), Lower Subansiri (99.23%), Papum Pare (98.05%), Tawang (98.64%), Tirap (94.66%), Upper Siang (98.94%), and West Siang (93.16%). Comparing the academic achievement of 10th grade students of government and private secondary schools of selected districts of Arunachal Pradesh, we find that the students of private secondary schools have performed better than that of government secondary schools.

Table 3.13: Year-Wise Trend Analysis of the Academic Achievement of the 10th Grade Students of Arunachal Pradesh during the Academic Sessions 2013-2018.

Year/ Academic Session	Category Achievement Score (%)	No. of Students obtained Score	Percentage (%)
2012-13	Below or equal to 40%	3374/13483	25.02%
	41% - 60%	7201	53.40%
	61% - 80%	2545	18.87%
	Above 80%	363	2.69%
2013-14	Below or equal to 40%	2320/12093	19.18%
	41% - 60%	8056	66.61%
	61% - 80%	1483	12.26%
	Above 80%	234	1.93%
2014-15	Below or equal to 40%	2879/15579	18.48%
	41% - 60%	9846	63.20%
	61% - 80%	1990	12.77%
	Above 80%	864	5.54%
2015-16	Below or equal to 40%	3860/14272	27.04%
	41% - 60%	8211	57.53%
	61% - 80%	1938	13.57%
	Above 80%	263	1.84%
2016-17	Below or equal to 40%	1038/12027	8.63%
	41% - 60%	7718	64.17%
	61% - 80%	2737	22.75%
	Above 80%	534	4.44%

2017-18	Below or equal to 40%	3321/14614	22.72%
	41% - 60%	7831	53.58%
	61% - 80%	3024	20.69%
	Above 80%	438	2.99%

Source: U-DISE (Unified District Information System for Education)

Interpretation: From the year-wise trend analysis, we find that in the academic session 2012-13, most (7,201) of the 10th grade students in Arunachal Pradesh in all types of management scored between 41% to 60% which was followed by 3,374 students who secured below or equal to 40% and 2,545 students securing between 61% to 80%. Only 363 10th grade students scored above 80% in the academic year 2012-13.

In the academic session 2013-14, most (8,056) of the 10th grade students in Arunachal Pradesh in all types of management scored between 41% to 60% which was followed by 2,320 students who secured below or equal to 40% and 1,483 students securing between 61% to 80%. Only 234 10th grade students scored above 80% in the academic year 2013-14.

In the academic session 2014-15, most (9846) of the 10th grade students in Arunachal Pradesh in all types of management scored between 41% to 60% which was followed by 2,879 students who secured below or equal to 40% and 1,990 students securing between 61% to 80%. Besides, 864 10th grade students scored above 80% in the academic year 2014-15.

The academic session 2015-16 reflects that the majority of the 10th grade students (8,211) in Arunachal Pradesh in all managements scored between 41% to 60%, followed by 3,860 students who secured below or equal to 40% and 1,938 students securing between 61% to 80%, and only 263 students secured above 80% in the academic year 2015-16.

In the academic session 2016-17, majority of the 10th grade students (7,718) in Arunachal Pradesh scored between 41% to 60%. 1,038 students scored below or equal to 40% and only 534 students scored above 80% in 2016-17.

Finally, in the academic session 2017-18, 7,831 10th grade students in Arunachal Pradesh scored between 41% to 60% and it was followed by 3,321 students securing below or equal to 40% and 3,024 students securing between 61% to 80% and only 438 students scored above 80% in the academic year 2017-18.

Hence, the academic results of 10th grade students in Arunachal Pradesh from 2013 to 2018 reveals that most of the students scored between 41% to 60% and very few students scored above 80% in all these academic years.

Table 3.14: Gender-wise Trend Analysis on the Academic Achievement of the 10th Grade Students during the Academic Sessions 2013-2018.

Category Achievement Score (%)	Boys		Girls	
	Frequency	Percentage	Frequency	Percentage
Below or equal to 40%	8587	21.04%	8205	20.38%
41% - 60%	24049	58.92%	23814	59.15%
61% - 80%	6786	16.62%	6931	17.21%
Above 80%	1390	3.40%	1306	3.24%
Average Performance	40812	50.02%	40256	50.48%

Source: U-DISE (Unified District Information System for Education)

Interpretation: The above table reveals the academic achievement of 10th grade secondary school students in all the managements. It compares the academic performance of both boys and girls from the academic sessions 2013 to 2018. 21.04% of boys in 10th grade scored below or equal to 40%, 58.92% of boys scored between 41% to 60%, 16.62% of boys scored between 61% to 80%, and only 3.40% of boys scored above 80%. On the other hand, 20.38% of girls in 10th grade scored below or equal to 40%, 59.15% of girls scored between 41% to 60%, 17.21% of girls scored between 61% to 80%, and only 3.24% of girls scored above 80%. If we combine the cases of boys and girls, it is found that majority of both the groups scored within the range of 41% to 60% and least of them scored above 80%. The average performance of the 10th grade secondary school boys is 50.02% and that of girls is 50.48%. Thus, girls at 10th grade performed a little better than the boys of the 10th grade in the secondary schools of Arunachal Pradesh.

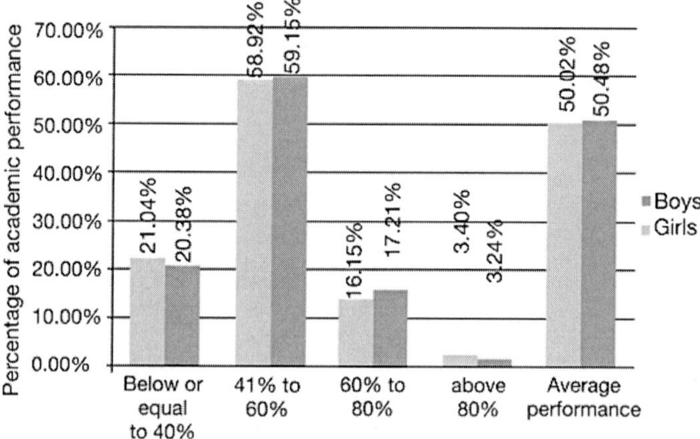

Figure 3.3: Gender-wise Trend Analysis on the Academic Achievement of the 10th Grade Students of Arunachal Pradesh during the Academic Sessions 2013-2018.

Objective VI. *To compare the academic achievement of 10th grade secondary school students of Arunachal Pradesh Before and After the removal of CCE pattern of Evaluation.*

Table 3.15: Academic achievement of 10th Grade Students before and after the removal of CCE pattern of Evaluation.

Category Achievement Score (%)	Before Removal of CCE (2014-15 & 2015-16)		After Removal of CCE (2016-17 & 2017-18)	
	Frequency	**Percentage**	**Frequency**	**Percentage**
Below or equal to 40%	6739	22.57%	4359	16.35%
41% - 60%	18057	60.49%	15549	58.36%
61% - 80%	3928	13.15%	5761	21.62%
Above 80%	1127	3.77%	972	3.64%
Average Performance	29851	50.87%	26641	47.99%

Source: U-DISE (Unified District Information System for Education)

Interpretation: The above table indicates the academic achievement of 10th grade secondary school students before and after the removal of CCE pattern of evaluation. The table explains that before the removal of CCE pattern of evaluation, 22.57% of the 10th grade secondary school students scored below or equal to 40%, 60.49% of the students scored between 41% to 60%, 13.15% of the students scored within the range of 61%-80%, and only 3.77% of the students secured above 80%

in the academic sessions 2014-15 and 2015-16. On the other hand, after the removal of CCE pattern of evaluation, 16.35% of the 10th grade secondary school students secured below or equal to 40%, 58.36% of the students secured between 41% to 60%, 21.62% of the students scored within the range of 61%-80%, and only 3.64% of the students secured above 80% in the academic sessions 2016-17 and 2017-18. Hence, before the removal of the CCE pattern of evaluation, most of the 10th grade students (18057) in the secondary schools secured within the range of 41%-60% and even after the removal of CCE pattern of evaluation most of the students (15549) secured within the range of 41%-60% in the academic sessions under observation. The average performance of the 10th grade secondary school students before the removal of CCE pattern was 50.87% and that of after the removal of CCE pattern was 47.99%. It reveals that the performance of 10th grade students was better before the removal of CCE pattern of evaluation. Thus, due to no detention policy, the academic achievement of 10th grade secondary students was slightly higher before the removal of CCE pattern of evaluation than after the removal of CCE system.

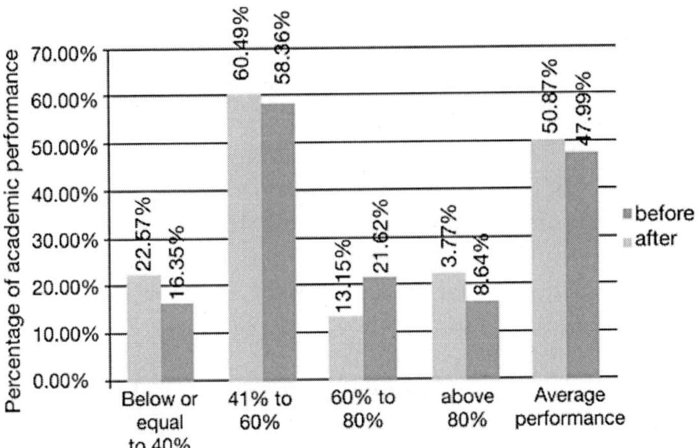

Figure 3.4: Academic Achievement of 10th Grade Students of Arunachal Pradesh before and after the removal of CCE pattern of evaluation.

It means that CCE is not a significant factor for the academic achievement of 10th grade students, as the quality of teaching learning was low during CCE pattern of evaluation. Therefore, CCE pattern was a failure in qualitative aspect which was ignored by the state Government during its implementation in the state and 'no detention' policy is better means for achieving better result at the secondary level.

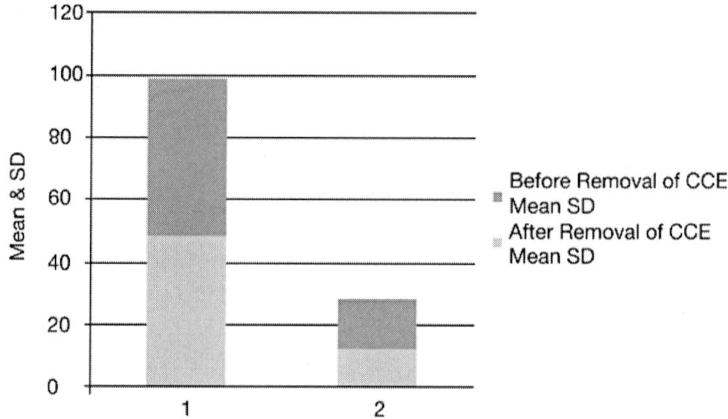

Figure 3.5: Academic Achievement of 10th Grade Students of Arunachal Pradesh before and after the removal of CCE pattern of evaluation.

Objective VII: *To find out the problems faced by Principals/ Headmasters, Teachers, and Students at Secondary Education in Arunachal Pradesh.*

This objective can be broken into three parts—(a) to investigate the problems faced by Headmasters/Principals of Secondary Schools; (b) to investigate the problems faced by Teachers of Secondary Schools; and (c) to investigate the problems faced by Students of Secondary Schools in Arunachal Pradesh. To investigate the problems faced by Headmasters/ Principals, Teachers, and the Students, the investigators have separated the management into Government and Private, and then interpretations have been made accordingly.

(a) To Investigate the problems faced by Headmasters/ Principals of Secondary Schools in Arunachal Pradesh.

The analysis and interpretations of the problems faced by Headmasters/Principals in the Government and Private Secondary Schools can be classified into three sections—(A) Teacher; (B) Curriculum, Co-Curricular Activities, Teaching-Learning, and Evaluation; and (C) Management, Finance, and Supervision. Besides, the descriptions of main problems faced by Headmasters/Principals in the Secondary Schools of Arunachal Pradesh are also provided.

Table 3.16: Percentage of response made by the Government and Private Secondary School Headmasters/Principals of Arunachal Pradesh relating to Section – A (Teacher).

Sl. No.	Items/Questions	Response	Govt. %	Pvt. %
1.	Are the numbers of teacher sufficient for your school?	Yes	60%	85%
		No	40%	15%
2.	Do you have sufficient number of science teachers?	Yes	35%	75%
		No	65%	25%
3.	Are the teachers punctual?	(a) Very punctual	70%	90%
		(b) Rarely punctual	20%	0%
		(c)Not punctual at all	10%	10%
4.	Are teachers committed towards profession?	(a) All are committed	45%	85%
		(b) Some are committed	45%	15%
		(c) Very few are committed	10%	0%
5.	Do the teachers use Teaching Learning Materials/ Teaching Aids in the classroom?	a) Very often	40%	65%
		b) Rarely use	25%	35%
		c) Never use	35%	0%
6.	Select the skilled manpower available in your school	a) Computer teacher	40%	75%
		b) Music teacher	15%	45%
		c) Sport teacher	35%	60%
		d) NCC/Scouts and Guides teacher	40%	30%
		e) Yoga teacher	0%	25%

Interpretation: The above table reveals the responses of the Headmasters/Principals regarding teacher-related problems in their schools. It indicates that:

- 40% of the government secondary school Headmasters/ Principals accepted that number of teachers are not sufficient in their schools whereas in case of private secondary school Headmasters/Principals, it is 15%.
- 65% of the government secondary school Headmasters/ Principals accepted that number of science teachers are not sufficient in their schools whereas in case of private secondary school Headmasters/Principals, it is 25%.
- 70% of the government secondary school Headmasters/ Principals accepted that teachers in their schools are very punctual, 20% rarely punctual, and 10% not punctual at all whereas 90% of private secondary school Headmasters/Principals accepted that teachers in their schools are very punctual and 10% not punctual at all.
- 45% of the government secondary school Headmasters/ Principals accepted that all the teachers in their schools are committed to their profession, 45% believe that some teachers are committed, and 10% think that very few teachers are committed whereas 85% of the private secondary school Headmasters/Principals accepted that all the teachers in their schools are committed to their profession and only 15% believe that some teachers are committed to their profession.
- 40% of the government secondary school Headmasters/ Principals accepted that teachers in their school use teaching learning materials/ teaching aids in the classrooms, 25% believe that teachers rarely use these technologies and 35% accepted that teachers in their schools never use these modern technologies whereas 65% of the private secondary school Headmasters/ Principals accepted that teachers in their schools use these modern technologies and only 35% believe that teachers in their schools rarely use these methods.

- 40% of the government secondary school Headmasters/Principals accepted to have computer teachers, 15% accepted to have music teachers, 35% accepted to have sport teachers, 40% accepted to have NCC/Scout Guide teachers and none accepted to have yoga teachers in their schools whereas 75% private secondary school Headmasters/Principals accepted to have computer teachers, 45% accepted to have music teachers, 60% accepted to have sport teachers, 30% accepted to have NCC/Scout Guide teachers, and 25% accepted to have yoga teachers in their schools.

Table 3.17: Responses of the Government and Private Secondary School Headmaster/Principals of Arunachal Pradesh relating to Section – B (Curriculum, Co-curricular activities, Teaching-Learning and Evaluation)

Sl. No.	Items/Questions	Response	Govt. %	Pvt. %
1.	Are you satisfied with the existing curriculum as per NCFSE 2005?	Yes	40%	75%
		No	55%	25%
2.	Is the existing curriculum relevant, productive, contextual and up-to-date?	Yes	80%	70%
		No	20%	30%
3.	Is the syllabus of secondary grade relevant to the present context?	Yes	70%	80%
		No	30%	20%
4.	Do you find any hard spots in the present curriculum?	Yes	15%	0%
		No	85%	100%
5.	Do you find difficulties in the implementation of RMSA scheme?	Yes	15%	5%
		No	85%	95%
6.	Does your school face problems in organizing Co-Curricular activities?	Yes	40%	15%
		No	60%	85%
7.	Does your school take your students to fieldtrips and excursion?	Yes	35%	65%
		No	65%	35%

Sl. No.	Items/Questions	Response	Govt. %	Pvt. %
8.	Are you satisfied with the attendance of the students of your school?	Yes	75%	85%
		No	25%	15%
9.	Are you satisfied with the academic performance of your students?	Yes	40%	70%
		No	60%	30%
10.	What is the medium of instruction mostly used by the teachers?	(a) English	35%	55%
		(b) Hindi	10%	0%
		(c) Mother-Tongue	5%	5%
		(d) Both Hindi and English	50%	40%
11.	What is the frequency assessment of students in your school?	(a) Weekly	15%	25%
		(b) Monthly	65%	55%
		(c) Quarterly	45%	25%
		(d) Half Yearly	35%	25%
		(e) Annually	35%	20%
12.	Which system of evaluation do you feel most appropriate for the teacher's attainment and holistic learning of the learners?	(a) CCE system	0%	20%
		(b) Existing external board exam	100%	80%

Interpretation: The above table reveals responses of the Headmasters/Principals regarding curriculum-related problems in their schools.

- 55% of the government secondary school Headmasters/Principals are not satisfied with the existing curriculum as per NCFSE 2005 whereas in case of private secondary school Headmasters/Principals it is 25%.
- 20% of the government secondary school Headmasters/Principals believe that the existing curriculum is not relevant, productive, contextual, and up-to-date, whereas in case of private secondary school Headmasters/Principals it is 30%.
- 30% of the government secondary school Headmasters/Principals believe that the syllabus of secondary grade

is not relevant to the present context whereas in case of private secondary school Headmasters/Principals it is 20%.

- 15% of the government secondary school Headmasters/Principals find hard spots in the present curriculum whereas in case of private secondary school Headmasters/Principals it is null, i.e., they do not find any hard spots in the present curriculum.
- 15% of the government secondary school Headmasters/Principals find difficulties in the implementation of RMSA scheme whereas only 5% private secondary school Headmasters/Principals find difficulties in the implementation of RMSA.
- 40% of the government secondary school Headmasters/Principals accepted that their schools face problems in organising co-curricular activities whereas in case of private secondary school Headmasters/Principals it is 15%.
- 65% of the government secondary school Headmasters/Principals accepted that their schools do not take students to field-trips and excursion whereas in case of private secondary school Headmasters/Principals it is 35%.
- 25% of the government secondary school Headmasters/Principals are not satisfied with the attendance of the students of their schools whereas in case of private secondary school Headmasters/Principals, it is 15%.
- 60% of the government secondary school Headmasters/Principals are not satisfied with the academic performance of their students whereas in case of private secondary school Headmasters/Principals, it is 30%.
- 35% of the government secondary school Headmasters/Principals accepted that the medium of instruction mostly used by their teachers is English, for 10%, it is Hindi, for 5%, it is Mother-Tongue, and 50% accepted both Hindi and English as the medium of instruction

whereas 55% of the private secondary school Headmasters/Principals accepted that the medium of instruction mostly used by their teachers is English, for 5%, it is Mother-Tongue, and 40% accepted both Hindi and English as the medium of instruction.

- 15% of the government secondary school Headmasters/ Principals accepted to have weekly assessment of students in their schools, 65% for monthly, 45% for quarterly, 35% for half-yearly, and 35% for annually assessment of students in their schools whereas 25% of private secondary school Headmasters/Principals accepted to have weekly assessment of students in their schools, 55% for monthly, 25% for quarterly, 25% for half-yearly, and 20% for annually assessment of students in their school.
- 100% of the government secondary school Headmasters/Principals are in favour of external board examination whereas 80% of the private secondary school Headmasters/Principals are in favour of external board examination and 20% in favour of CCE pattern of evaluation.

Table 3.18: Responses of the Government and Private Secondary School Headmasters/Principals of Arunachal Pradesh relating to Section – C (Management, Finance, and Supervision)

Sl. No.	Items/Questions	Response	Govt. %	Pvt. %
1.	Are the school SMC members supportive?	Yes	90%	80%
		No	10%	20%
2.	Does your school have institutional planning?	Yes	75%	70%
		No	25%	30%
3.	Are the school accounts audited annually?	Yes	90%	85%
		No	25%	15%
4.	Do you get financial assistance on time?	Yes	45%	55%
		No	55%	45%

Sl. No.	Items/Questions	Response	Govt. %	Pvt. %
5.	In a month, how many times do you hold staff meeting?	(a) Once	15%	30%
		(b) Twice	0%	10%
		(c) Weekly	5%	0%
		(d) Whenever necessary	55%	35%
6.	Who prepare the school budget?	(a) Director	5%	5%
		(b) Principal	25%	20%
		(c) SMC	15%	30%
		(d) DDSE	25%	10%
7.	How do you prepare your school budget?	(a) Annually	70%	70%
		(b) Half yearly	10%	0%
		(c) None	15%	30%
8.	Who visits for your school inspection?	(a) CBSE team	10%	30%
		(b) State Govt. Officials	55%	45%
		(c) Third party monitoring	0%	20%
9.	How many times does the inspection/ monitoring team visits to your school annually?	(a) Frequently	35%	10%
		(b) Periodically	55%	70%
		(c) Never visit	10%	5%
10.	Select the records/ register maintained by your school.	(a) Teachers' attendance	100%	100%
		(b) Students' register	100%	95%
		(c) Admission register	100%	95%
		(d) CRC record	25%	30%
		(e) Staff Meeting record	90%	85%
		(f) PTA meeting	70%	75%
		(g) Store log book	55%	65%
11.	What are the main financial sources of your school?	(a) Fully state government aid	75%	10%
		(b) Central government aid	15%	0%
		(c) Donation	0%	0%
		(d) School fees	25%	70%
		(e) Any other grant	5%	10%

Interpretation: The above table reveals responses of the Headmasters/Principals regarding problems related to management, finance, and supervision in their schools.

- 90% of government secondary school Headmasters/ Principals accepted that the School Management Committee (SMC) are supportive whereas in case of private secondary school Headmasters/Principals, it is 80%.
- 75% of government secondary school Headmasters/ Principals accepted to have institutional planning for their schools whereas in case of private secondary school Headmasters/Principals, it is 70%.
- 90% of government secondary school Headmasters/ Principals said that their accounts are audited annually whereas in case of private secondary school Headmasters/Principals, it is 85%.
- 45% of government secondary school Headmasters/ Principals accepted to get financial assistance for their schools on time whereas in case of private secondary school Headmasters/Principals, it is 55%.
- 15% of government secondary school Headmasters/ Principals accepted to hold staff meeting once in a month, 25% twice a month, 5% weekly, and 55% whenever necessary whereas 30% of private secondary school Headmasters/Principals accepted to hold staff meeting once in a month, 10% twice a month, 25% weekly, and 35% whenever necessary.
- 5% of government secondary school Headmasters/ Principals said that Director prepares the school budget, 25% principal, 15% SMC, and 25% DDSE whereas 5% of the private secondary school Headmasters/ Principals said that Director prepares the school budget, 20% principal, 30% SMC, and 10% DDSE.
- 70% of government secondary school Headmasters/ Principals said that they prepare their school budget annually, 10% half-yearly, and 15% said that they do not prepare their school budget whereas 70% of private secondary school Headmasters/Principals said that they prepare their school budget annually and 30% said that they do not prepare their school budget.

- 45% of government secondary school Headmasters/ Principals said that CBSE team makes inspection of their schools and 55% said that state government officials make inspection of their schools whereas 30% of private secondary school Headmasters/Principals said that CBSE team makes inspection of their schools, 45% said state government officials, and 25% said that third party makes monitoring of their schools.
- 35% of government secondary school Headmasters/ Principals informed that the inspection/monitoring team visits their school frequently, 55% periodically, and 10% said that inspection/monitoring team never visits their school whereas 10% of private secondary school Headmasters/Principals informed that the inspection/ monitoring team visits their school frequently, 70% periodically, and 20% said inspection/monitoring team never visits their schools.
- All the government secondary school Headmasters/ Principals admitted to maintain teachers' attendance register, students' register, and admission register; 25% said that they keep CRC record; 90% said that they maintain staff meeting record; 70% said that they maintain PTA meeting record; and 55% said that they maintain store log book; whereas all the private secondary school Headmasters/Principals admitted to maintain teachers' attendance register; 95% said that they maintain students' register; 95% said that they maintain admission register; 30% said that they keep CRC record; 85% said that they maintain staff meeting record; 75% said that they maintain PTA meeting record; and 65% said that they keep the record of store log book.
- 75% of government secondary school Headmasters/ Principals admitted that their main financial source is state government aid, for 15% schools central government aid, for 5% schools fees, and 5% said that they get various other grants whereas 10% of private

secondary school Headmasters/Principals admitted that their main financial source is state government aid, for 70% school fees, and 20% said that they get various other grants.

Table 3.19: Main problems faced by the Headmasters/Principals in the Government Secondary Schools of Arunachal Pradesh

Sl. No.	Main problems faced by the Headmasters/Principals in the Government Secondary Schools
1.	Late posting of subject teachers
2.	Overcrowded classrooms, Indiscipline in the school
3.	Lack of resources such as furniture, teaching aids, school boundary, laboratory, auditorium, quarter, Untimely supply of textbooks etc.
4.	Sanitation problem, Improper electrical wiring
5.	Lack of moral responsibility on the part of teachers
6.	Lack of clerical personnel and shortage of group D staffs
7.	Absence of proper playground, No facilities for games and sports
8.	Insufficient fund by the state government
9.	Poor SMC attendance and time management problem among SMC members

Interpretation: Main problems faced by the Headmasters/ Principals in the Government Secondary Schools are: Late posting of subject teachers, Indiscipline in the school, Lack of resources such as furniture, teaching aids, school boundary, laboratory, auditorium, quarter etc., Sanitation problem, Overcrowded classrooms, Lack of moral responsibility on the part of teachers, Lack of clerical personnel and shortage of group D staffs, Improper electrical wiring, Absence of proper playground, No facilities for games and sports, Untimely supply of textbooks, Insufficient fund by the state government, Poor SMC attendance and time management problem among SMC members, and so on.

On the other hand, main problems faced by Headmasters/ Principals in the Private Secondary Schools of Arunachal Pradesh include: No motivation given to students, No proper supply of textbooks, No cooperation, Absence of medical facility,

Difficulty in arrangement of teachers, Lack of library, science laboratory, good furniture, etc., No help from government both state and central, Irregularity of students, and Lack of interest on the part of teachers.

(b) To Investigate the Problems faced by Teachers of Secondary Schools in Arunachal Pradesh.

The analysis and interpretations of the problems faced by teachers in the government and private secondary schools have been classified into three sections—(A) Teaching Profession, (B) Academic, Curriculum, and Evaluation, and (C) Management and Administration. Besides, the descriptions of main problems faced by teachers in the secondary schools of Arunachal Pradesh are also provided.

Table 3.20: Responses of the Government and Private Secondary School Teachers of Arunachal Pradesh relating to Section – A (Teaching Profession)

Sl. No.	Items/Questions	Response	Govt. %	Pvt. %
1.	Are you satisfied with the teaching job at Secondary School Level?	Yes	90.90%	90%
		No	9.09%	10%
2.	Are you committed to Teaching Profession?	(a) Very much committed	73.98%	69.25%
		(b) Average	49.64%	23.33%
		(c) Not committed	4.38%	7.40%
3.	Are you Punctual?	(a) Very much punctual	87.77%	82.22%
		(b) Sometimes	10.97%	11.85%
		(c) Not punctual at all	1.25%	5.92%
4.	Do you follow Code of Ethics of your profession?	Yes	93.10%	86.66%
		No	6.89%	13.33%
5.	Are you interested in organizing Seminar/ Conference/ Research work?	Yes	83.38%	88.88%
		No	16.61%	11.11%
6.	Are you aware of RTE Act and its intervention?	Yes	89.34%	85.18%
		No	10.65%	14.81%

Sl. No.	Items/Questions	Response	Govt. %	Pvt. %
7.	Have you undergone some training for RTE Act?	Yes	28.21%	26.29%
		No	71.78%	73.70%

Interpretation: The above table indicates that:

- 90% of both government and private secondary school teachers are satisfied with the teaching job at secondary school level.
- 73.98% of government secondary school teachers claimed that they are very much committed to teaching profession, 21.64% are averagely committed, and 4.38% are not committed to teaching profession at all, whereas 69.25% of private secondary school teachers claimed that they are very much committed to teaching profession, 23.33% are averagely committed, and 7.4% are not committed to teaching profession at all.
- 87.77% of government secondary school teachers claimed that they are punctual, 10.97% sometimes, and only 1.25% declared that they are not punctual at all, whereas 82.22% of private secondary school teachers claimed that they are punctual, 11.85% sometimes, and only 5.92% declared that they are not punctual at all.
- 93.10% of government secondary school teachers said to have followed the code of ethics of their profession, whereas in case of private secondary school teachers, it is 86.66%.
- 16.61% of government secondary school teachers displayed disinterest in organizing seminar/conference/research work, whereas in case of private secondary school teachers, it is 11.11%.
- 89.34% of government secondary school teachers are aware of RTE act and its intervention, whereas in case of private secondary school teachers, it is 85.18%.

- 28.21% of government secondary school teachers have undergone training for RTE Act, whereas in case of private secondary school teachers, it is 26.29%.

Table 3.21: Responses of the Government and Private Secondary School Teachers of Arunachal Pradesh relating to Section – B (Academic, Curriculum, and Evaluation)

Sl. No.	Items/Questions	Response	Govt. %	Pvt. %
1.	Are you satisfied with the existing Curriculum as per NCFSE 2005?	Yes	65.83%	71.48%
		No	34.16%	28.51%
2.	Are the text books relevant, up-to- date and suitable to the need of the students?	Yes	68.33%	92.59%
		No	31.66%	7.40%
3.	Is the syllabus of secondary grade emphasizing skilled based knowledge?	Yes	72.10%	81.11%
		No	27.89%	18.88%
4.	Do you manage to complete your syllabi on time?	Yes	92.47%	100%
		No	7.52%	0%
5.	Do you find difficulties in the implementation of RMSA scheme?	Yes	16.61%	6.29%
		No	83.38%	93.70%
6.	Are you satisfied with the attendance & performance of the students?	Yes	47.64%	74.81%
		No	52.35%	25.18%
7.	Are you comfortable to take classes in the smart classroom?	Yes	30.09%	32.59%
		No	69.90%	67.40%
8.	Are you familiar with CAI?	Yes	46.39%	47.77%
		No	53.60%	52.22%
9.	Do you use Teaching Learning Materials/ Teaching aids in the classroom?	(a) Very Often	49.28%	52.96%
		(b) Rarely	40.75%	35.18%
		(c) Never	10.03%	11.85%

Sl. No.	Items/Questions	Response	Govt. %	Pvt. %
10.	Which method of teaching do you mostly use in the classroom?	(a) Lecture cum Demonstration	42.94%	25.92%
		(b) Project method,	2.82%	4.44%
		(c) Experimental and Inductive deductive,	4.70%	4.44%
		(d) Illustration method	1.56%	4.81%
		(e) Discussion	12.85%	9.25%
		(f) Story Telling	6.58%	9.25%
		(g) Question-Answer	1.88%	4.44%
11.	What Medium of Instruction do you mostly use in the classroom?	(a) English	25.39%	68.88%
		(b) Hindi	9.71%	4.44%
		(c) Mother-Tongue	4.38%	2.22%
		(d) Both English & Hindi	60.50%	24.44%
12.	Which system of evaluation do you feel most appropriate for the holistic learning of the learners?	(a) CCE system	10.34%	24.81%
		(b) Existing external board exam	89.65%	75.18%

Interpretation: The above table indicates that:

- 65.83% of government secondary school teachers are satisfied with the existing curriculum as per NCFSE 2005, whereas in case of private secondary school teachers, it is 71.48%.
- 68.33% of government secondary school teachers consider textbook to be relevant, up-to-date, and suitable to the needs of the students, whereas in case of private secondary school teachers, it is 92.59%.
- 72.10% of government secondary school teachers declared that the syllabus of the secondary grade is emphasizing skilled based knowledge, whereas in case of private secondary school teachers, it is 81.11%.
- 92.47% of government secondary school teachers claimed to complete their syllabi on time, whereas in case of private secondary school teachers, it is 100%.

- 16.61% of government secondary school teachers find difficulties in the implementation of RMSA scheme, whereas in case of private secondary school teachers, it is 6.29%.
- 52.35% of government secondary school teachers are not satisfied with the attendance and performance of the students, whereas in case of private secondary school teachers, it is 25.18%.
- 69.90% of government secondary school teachers are not comfortable to take classes in smart classrooms, whereas in case of private secondary school teachers, it is 67.40%.
- 53.60% of government secondary school teachers are not familiar with Computer-Assisted Instruction (CAI), whereas in case of private secondary school teachers, it is 52.22%.
- 49.25% of government secondary school teachers very often use Teaching Learning Materials/Teaching Aids in the classrooms, 40.75% rarely, and 10.03% never use these methods, whereas 52.96% of private secondary school teachers very often use these methods, 35.18% rarely, and 11.85% never use these methods in the classrooms.
- Teaching method mostly used in the classrooms by the government secondary school teachers are: lecture cum demonstration – 42.94%, project method – 28.20%, experimental and inductive/deductive – 4.70%, illustration method – 1.56%, discussion method – 12.85%, story telling – 6.58%, and question-answer method – 1.88%, whereas in case of private secondary school teachers these are: lecture cum demonstration – 25.92%, project method – 44.40%, experimental and inductive/deductive – 4.44%, illustration method – 4.81%, discussion method – 9.25%, story telling – 9.25%, and question-answer method – 4.44%.
- Most of the teachers (60.50%) in the government secondary schools use both English and Hindi as the

medium of instruction in the classrooms, whereas most of the teachers (68.88%) in the private secondary schools use English as the medium of instruction in the classrooms.

- 89.65% of government secondary school teachers prefer the existing external board exam as the most appropriate system for the holistic learning of the learners and 10.34% prefer CCE pattern of evaluation, whereas 75.18% of private secondary school teachers prefer existing external board exam and 24.81% prefer CCE pattern of evaluation.

Table 3.22: Response of the Government and Private Secondary School Teachers of Arunachal Pradesh relating to Section – C (Management and Administration)

Sl. No.	Items/Questions	Response	Govt. %	Pvt. %
1.	Is Head-in Charge of your school cooperative and Regular?	Yes	93.10%	95.55%
		No	6.89%	4.44%
2.	Does the inspection team visit your school regularly?	Yes	46.39%	32.22%
		No	53.60%	67.77%
3.	Do you get sufficient leave for attending In-Service Training Programme?	Yes	83.38%	86.66%
		No	16.61%	13.33%
4.	Does your school have a grievances mechanism/ anti corporal punishment cell?	Yes	13.16%	30%
		No	86.83%	70%
5.	Does your school authority collect extra fees from the students?	Yes	9.40%	11.11%
		No	90.59%	88.88%

6.	Do you express your opinion freely before your authority?	Yes	89.02%	80.74%
		No	10.97%	19.25%
7.	Do you face problem in the release of convergence grant from the school?	Yes	26.33%	15.81%
		No	73.66%	84.81%
8.	Do you use teaching skills efficiently while teaching in the classroom?	Yes	99.37%	93.33%
		No	0.62%	6.66%
9.	What are the common problems among the students?	(a) Indiscipline	57.05%	54.44%
		(b) Addicted to drug/bad eating habits	9.09%	2.59%
		(c) Internet/mobile addiction	19.12%	12.22%
		(d) Indecent dress	16.92%	15.92%
10.	Select the area in which you mostly face problems	(a) Poor salary	28.84%	44.81%
		(b) Heavy workload	22.57%	18.88%
		(c) Lack of quarter	33.85%	9.62%
		(d) Syllabus completion	9.40%	11.48%
		(e) Dealing with slow learners	39.81%	47.03%
		(f) Over crowded class	37.30%	14.44%
		(g) Lesson planning	6.58%	6.29%
11.	How many times in a month does your school hold staff meeting?	(a) Frequently	19.43%	53.70%
		(b) Sometimes	74.29%	44.81%
		(c) Never	6.26%	1.48%
12.	Who visits for the school inspection?	(a) CBSE Team	6.89%	17.77%
		(b) State Govt. Officials	67.39%	23.70%
		(c) School management team	32.91%	51.85%
13.	How often does the inspection team visit your school?	(a) Frequency	15.36%	15.55%
		(b) Periodically	68.33%	61.48%
		(c) Never	16.30%	22.96%

14.	In organization of which of the activities do you face difficulty?	(a) Workshop/Seminar/ Conference	15.67%	11.48%
		(b) Career counseling	19.43%	17.40%
		(c) Sports events	5.95%	10%
		(d) Field trips/Excursion	35.10%	18.88%
		(e) Literary events	5.32%	1.85%
		(f) Assembly events	7.83%	4.07%
		(g) NCC/Scouts and Guides	5.95%	17.03%
15.	In following which of the records do you face difficulty?	(a) Admission Register	2.50%	7.40%
		(b) Cumulative Record Card	9.71%	12.59%
		(c) PTA meeting records	15.04%	7.40%
		(d) Store Logbook	4.38%	4.07%
		(e) Staff meeting records	2.50%	1.48%
		(f) Science Lab	13.47%	7.03%
		(g) Time table	6.26%	6.29%
16.	Give reasons for deteriorating of secondary schools in Arunachal Pradesh	(a) Lack of trained teachers	15.36%	42.59%
		(b) Poor infrastructure	51.09%	45.92%
		(c) Poor quality teaching	14.42%	47.77%
		(d) Irrelevant curriculum	15.04%	18.88%
		(e) Frequent change of education policy	36.05%	28.88%
		(f) Lack of funds	28.84%	23.70%
		(g) Lack of Science teachers	31.97%	20.74%
		(h) Lack of incentives	16.92%	20%
		(i) Insufficient teachers	51.72%	34.81%
		(j) Lack of innovation	26.95%	34.44%
		(k) Political interference	26.01%	24.44%
		(l) Poor monitoring	51.10%	47.77%

Interpretation: The above table indicates that:

- 93.10% of government secondary school teachers claimed that their head-in-charge are cooperative and regular, whereas in case of private secondary school teachers, it is 95.55%.

- 53.69% of government secondary school teachers accepted that inspection team does not visit their schools regularly, whereas in case of private secondary schools, it is 67.77%.
- 83.38% of government secondary school teachers claimed that they get sufficient leave for attending in-service training programme, whereas in case of private secondary school teachers, it is 86.66%.
- 86.83% of government secondary school teachers accepted that their schools do not have grievance mechanism/anti corporal punishment cells, whereas in case of private secondary school teachers, it is 70%.
- 90.59% of government secondary school teachers revealed that their school authorities do to collect extra fees from the students, whereas in case of private secondary school, it is 88.88%.
- 89.02% of government secondary school teachers express their opinion freely before their authorities, whereas in case of private secondary school teachers, it is 80.74%.
- 73.66% of government secondary school teachers responded that they do not face any problem in releasing convergence grant from their school, whereas in case of private secondary school teachers, it is 84.81%.
- 99.37% of the government secondary school teachers claimed that they use teaching skills efficiently while teaching in the classroom, whereas in case of private secondary school teachers, it is 93.33%.
- 57.05% of the government secondary school teachers found indiscipline as the most common problems among the students, 9.09% found drug addiction/bad eating habits as the common problems, 19.12% found internet/mobile addiction as the common problems, and 16.92% found indecent dress as the common problems among the students, whereas 54.44% of the private secondary school teachers found indiscipline

as the most common problems among the students, 2.59% found drug addiction/bad eating habits as the common problems, 12.22% found internet/mobile addiction as the common problems, and 15.92% found indecent dress as the common problems among the students.

- 28.84% of the government secondary school teachers complained for their poor salary, 22.57% for heavy workload, 33.85% for lack of quarters, 9.40% for syllabus completion, 39.81% for dealing with slow learners, 37.30% for overcrowded classrooms, and 6.58% for lesson planning, whereas 44.81% of the private secondary school teachers complained for their poor salary, 18.88% for heavy work load, 9.62% for lack of quarters, 11.48% for syllabus completion, 47.03% for dealing with slow learners, 14.44% for overcrowded class, and 6.29% for lesson planning.
- 19.43% of government secondary school teachers accepted to have frequent staff meetings in a month in their schools, 74.29% of them said that staff meetings are held sometimes in a month, and 6.26% said that staff meetings never held in their schools, whereas 53.70% of private secondary school teachers accepted to have frequent staff meetings in a month in their schools, 44.81% of them said that staff meetings are held sometimes in a month, and 1.48% said that staff meetings never held in their schools.
- 6.89% of government secondary school teachers said that CBSE team visits their schools for inspection, 67.39% of them said State Government Officials, and 32.91% said that school management team does inspection of their schools, whereas 17.77% of private secondary school teachers said that CBSE team visits their schools for inspection, 23.70% of them said State Government Officials, and 51.85% said that school management team does inspection of their schools.
- 15.36% of government secondary school teachers accepted that the inspection team visits their schools

frequently, 68.33% said periodically, and 16.30% said that the inspection team never visits their schools, whereas 15.55% of private secondary school teachers accepted that the inspection team visits their schools frequently, 61.48% said periodically, and 22.96% said that the inspection team never visits their schools.

- Most of the government secondary school teachers face difficulty in organizing field trips/excursion (35.10%), followed by career counselling (19.43%), workshop/seminar/conference (15.67%), assembly events (7.83%), sports events (5.95%), NCC/Scouts and Guides (5.95%), and literary events (5.32%), whereas most of the private secondary school teachers face difficulty in organizing field trip/excursion (18.88%), followed by career counselling (17.40%), NCC/Scouts and Guides (17.03%), workshop/seminar/conference (11.48%), sports events (10%), assembly events (4.07%), and literary events (1.85%).
- Most of the government secondary school teachers face difficulty in keeping the records of PTA meetings (15.04%), followed by Science lab (13.47%), cumulative record card (9.71%), time table (6.26%), store logbook (4.38%), and admission register and staff meeting records (2.5% each), whereas most of the private secondary school teachers face difficulty in keeping the records of cumulative record card (12.59%), followed by admission register and PTA meetings (7.40% each), Science lab (7.03%), time table (6.29%), store logbook (4.07%), and staff meeting records (1.48%).
- Reasons for deterioration of secondary schools in Arunachal Pradesh are more or less same as per both the government and private secondary school teachers. Primary reasons given by them are: lack of trained teachers, poor infrastructure, poor quality of teasing, irrelevant curriculum, frequent change of education policy, lack of funds, lack of science teachers, lack

of incentives, insufficient teachers, lack of innovation, political interferences, and poor monitoring.

Along with the above common problems faced by the teachers in the government secondary schools, they face some acute problems in their profession. Despite drawing good salary and having a secured job, the government secondary school teachers serving in various districts of Arunachal Pradesh are not satisfied with the posting areas, particularly in the rural areas, because of lack of infrastructure facilities, proper and hygienic toilets, clean drinking water facilities, and quarter facilities; overburden administration, additional tasks other than teaching, additional periods assigned to them on non-specialized subjects, and so on.

Whereas, the main problems faced by the teachers of the private secondary schools are: poor salary for teachers, late disbursement of salary, lack of Science and Hindi teachers, lack of trained teachers, lack of unity among teachers, lack of teachers' quarters, shortage of subject teachers, frequent change of teachers in the school, inadequate school library and laboratory, lack of coordination between teachers and the managing team, no proper school planning, no internet connectivity, commercialization of education, indiscipline dress code, students' indiscipline, no professional status given to teachers, teachers' innovative ideas are not supported by the officials and teachers' suggestions are not considered, no regular PTA meeting conducted in the school, no proper toilet rooms and safe drinking water facility, discrimination between government and private school teachers, school routine and calendar does not meet national needs, and no work balance and lack of motivation for professional development of teachers.

While reflecting on the above problems of private secondary school teachers, it is observed that although they enjoy better facilities than the government secondary school teachers, yet most of the private secondary school teachers are not satisfied with their profession.

The highlighted severe problems faced by the teachers in the private secondary schools include heavy workload, low salary and high expectation, job insecurity, and discrimination between government and private school teachers. These are some of the factors which hamper overall inputs towards the progress of students' performance and in the presence of such causes of dissatisfaction among the private school teachers, overall development of school is not possible.

(c) To Investigate the Problems faced by Students of Secondary Schools in Arunachal Pradesh.

The analysis and interpretations of the problems faced by students in the government and private secondary schools have been classified into four sections—(A) Teacher related problem, (B) Student related problem, (C) Co-Curricular, and (D) Others. Besides, descriptions of the main problems faced by Students in the secondary schools of Arunachal Pradesh have been provided.

Table 3.23: Responses of the Government and Private Secondary School Students of Arunachal Pradesh relating to Section – A (Teacher related Problems).

Sl. No.	Items/Questions	Response	Govt. %	Pvt.%
1.	Are you satisfied with the teaching-learning process in your school?	Yes	65.86%	63.67%
		No	34.13%	36.32%
2.	Are your teachers punctual?	(a) Punctual	30.17%	50.68%
		(b) Sometimes	62.07%	45.86%
		(c) Not punctual at all	7.74%	3.44%
3.	Does your school provide resource teachers?	(a) Computer teacher	34.70%	65.17%
		(b) Music teacher	7.00%	18.16%
		(c) Sport teacher	46.82%	43.33%
		(d) NCC/Scouts and Guides	49.87%	28.96%
		(e) Yoga teacher	6.67%	8.04%
4.	Does your teacher use teaching-learning materials/ teaching aids?	(a) Very Often	15.91%	22.87%
		(b) Rarely	37.34%	60.11%
		(c) Never	46.74%	17.01%
5.	What type of teaching aids does your teacher use in classroom?	(a) Maps/Globes	19.95%	41.26%
		(b) Charts	15.00%	35.28%
		(c) Models,	9.64%	18.39%
		(d) Encyclopedia	26.54%	38.27%
		(e) No teaching aids	44.84%	42.98%

6.	Do your teachers complete your syllabi on time?	Yes	43.52%	61.14%
		No	56.47%	38.85%
7.	What method do your teachers mostly use in your classroom?	(a) Lecture cum Demonstration	73.78%	83.21%
		(b) Project method,	30.25%	38.27%
		(c) Experimental and Inductive deductive,	5.93%	13.33%
		(d) Illustration method	22.25%	10.11%
8.	What is the medium of instruction mostly used by your teachers?	(a) English	5.35%	47.47%
		(b) Hindi	19.20%	2.52%
		(c) Mother tongue	4.28%	0.22%
		(d) Hindi & English	71.14%	49.77%

Interpretation: The above table reveals that:

- 65.86% of the government secondary school students are satisfied with the teaching-learning process of their schools, whereas in case of private secondary school students, it is 63.67%.
- 30.17% of government secondary school students accepted that their teachers are punctual, 62.07% said that their teachers are sometime punctual, and only 7.74% think that their teachers are not punctual at all, whereas 50.68% of private secondary school students accepted that their teachers are punctual, 45.86% said that their teachers are sometime punctual, and only 3.44% think that their teachers are not punctual at all.
- 34.70% of the government secondary school students accepted to have computer teachers, 7% accepted to have music teachers, 46.82% accepted to have sport teachers, 49.87% accepted to have NCC/Scouts and Guides, and only 6.67% accepted to have yoga teachers in their schools, whereas 65.17% of private secondary school students accepted to have computer teachers, 18.16% accepted to have music teachers, 43.33% accepted to have sport teachers, 28.96%

accepted to have NCC/Scouts and Guides, and only 8.09% accepted to have yoga teachers in their schools.

- Most of the government secondary school students accepted that their teachers never use teaching learning materials/teaching aids, whereas most of the private secondary school students accepted that their teachers rarely use these modern methods. 15.91% of the government secondary school students and 22.87% of the private secondary school students accepted that their teachers very often use these modern methods.
- Majority of government and private secondary school students accepted that their teachers use teaching aids, such as maps/globs, charts, models, encyclopedia, etc. in the classrooms. 44.84% of government secondary school students and 42.98% of private secondary school students accepted that their teachers do not use any kind of teaching aids.
- Majority of government secondary school students (56.47%) accepted that their teachers do not complete their syllabi on time whereas majority of private secondary school students (61.14) accepted that their teachers complete their syllabi on time.
- Majority of government and private secondary school students accepted that their teachers mostly use lecture cum demonstration method of teaching in their classrooms. Only 5.93% of government secondary school students and 13.33% of private secondary school students accepted that their teachers use experimental and inductive/deductive methods of teaching in their classrooms.
- Majority of government and private secondary students accepted that their teachers mostly use Hindi and English as the medium of instruction in the classrooms. Only 5.35% of government and 47.47% of private secondary school students accepted that their teachers use English as the medium of instruction in the classrooms. Mother tongue as medium of instruction is

rarely used in government as well as private secondary schools.

Table 3.24: Response of the Government and Private Secondary School Students of Arunachal Pradesh relating to Section – B (Student related Problems)

Sl. No.	Items/Questions	Response	Govt. %	Pvt. %
1.	Do you attend school regularly?	Yes	86.89%	90.11%
		No	13.10%	9.88%
2.	Reasons for facing difficulty in understanding the lessons taught by your teachers	(a) No subject knowledge	7.50%	7.47%
		(b) Lack clarity in explanation	25.96%	35.28%
		(c) Lack legibility in handwriting	15.82%	5.28%
		(d) Communication/Language problem	16.07%	17.93%
		(e) Not using teaching aids	25.06%	25.51%
3.	In which subject do you mostly face difficulty in learning?	(a) Math	45.67%	46.20%
		(b) Science	41.46%	34.82%
		(c) Hindi	16.32%	29.54%
		(d) English	9.81%	8.39%
		(e) Social Science	26.62%	16.89%

Interpretation: The above table indicates that:

- Majority of government and private secondary school students attend their school regularly. 86.89% of government and 90.11% of private secondary school students attend their schools regularly.
- 25.96% of government secondary school students accepted lack of clarity in explanation, 25.06% not using of teaching aids, 16.67% communication/ language problem, 15.82% lack of legibility in handwriting, and 7.50% lack of subject knowledge as the main reasons for facing difficulty in understanding the lessons taught by their teachers, whereas 35.28% of private secondary school students accepted lack of clarity in explanation, 25.51% not using of teaching aids, 17.93% communication/language problem, 5.28% lack of legibility in handwriting, and 7.47%

lack of subject knowledge as the main reasons for facing difficulty in understanding the lessons taught by their teachers in the classroom.

- Most of the government and private secondary school students mostly face difficulty in learning Maths and Science. 45.67% of government secondary school students face difficulty in learning maths and 41.46% in science, whereas 46.20% of private secondary school students face difficulty in learning maths and 34.82% in science.

Table 3.25: Responses of the Government and Private Secondary School Students of Arunachal Pradesh relating to Section – C (Co-curricular Activities)

Sl. No.	Items	Govt.%	Pvt. %
1.	Football	75.68%	74.82%
2.	Basketball	2.80%	31.14%
3.	Volleyball	54.65%	67.24%
4.	Table Tennis	1.23%	12.98%
5.	Badminton	23.49%	49.08%
6.	Cricket	18.54%	19.31%
7.	Debate	25.96%	62.06%
8.	Seminar	42.12%	61.60%
9.	Quiz	71.80%	81.37%
10.	Exhibition	14.01%	54.13%
11.	Drawing and Painting	71.64%	91.60%
12.	Extempore Speech	59.85%	85.63%
13.	Drama	42.62%	77.01%
14.	Singing	67.18%	92.06%
15.	Dancing	78.07%	97.58%
16.	Attire Show	18.30%	35.63%
17.	Instrumental	6.26%	23.21%
18.	Mime play	4.36%	19.08%

Interpretation: Out of the 18 co-curricular activities listed above, the government secondary schools organize dancing (78.07%), football (75.68%), and singing (67.18%) at the most, whereas students get least opportunities in activities, such as table tennis (1.23%), basketball (2.80%), mime play (4.36%), instrumental (6.26%), exhibition (14.01%), debate (25.96%), badminton (23.49%), cricket (18.54%), and seminars (42.12%) in their schools. Thus, it reflects that most of the government secondary schools are not encouraging co-curricular activities due to shortage of proper playgrounds and lack of physical sport teachers, and not organizing recreation activities for all round development of the students at this stage.

Whereas, the private secondary schools organize dancing (97.58%), singing (92.06%), drawing and painting (91.60%), quiz (81.37%), seminar (61.60%), debate (62.06%), and extempore speech (85.63%) at the most. And at the least, they have table tennis (12.98%) and mime play (19.08%) in their schools. However, the private secondary schools organize all the above listed co-curricular activities.

Table 3.26: Responses of the Government and Private Secondary School Students of Arunachal Pradesh relating to Section – D (Others)

Sl. No.	Items	Response	Govt.%	Pvt. %
1.	Does your school implement 'Swachh Bharat Abhiyan'?	Yes	79.63%	79.88%
		No	20.36%	20.11%
2.	Do you feel that your school create social discrimination atmosphere?	Yes	13.52%	20.68%
		No	86.47%	79.31%
3.	Does your school pressurize to play or sit only with the same gender?	Yes	13.60%	28.27%
		No	86.39%	71.72%
4.	Is the syllabus of the secondary grade relevant to the present context?	Yes	61.25%	78.73%
		No	38.74%	21.26%
5.	Which system of evaluation do you feel most appropriate for the holistic learning of the learners?	(a) CCE system	37.67%	46.89%
		(b) Existing external board exam	62.32%	53.10%

Interpretation: The above table shows the responses of students on the problems faced by them in the government and private secondary schools of Arunachal Pradesh.

- 79.63% of government and 79.88% of private secondary school students accepted that their schools have implemented the "Swachh Bharat Abhiyan".
- 86.47% of government and 79.31% of private secondary school students feel that their schools do not create social discrimination atmosphere.
- 86.39% of government and 71.72% of private secondary school students accepted that their schools do not pressurize to play or sit only with the same gender.
- 61.25% of government and 78.73% of private secondary school students believe that the syllabus of the secondary grade is relevant to the present context.
- 62.32% of government and 53.10% of private secondary school students believe that external board exam system of evaluation is the most appropriate for the holistic learning of the learners. On the other hand, 37.67% of government and 46.89% of private secondary school students favour CCE system of evaluation.

Table 3.27: Main problems faced by the Students in the Government Secondary Schools of Arunachal Pradesh

Sl. No.	Main Problems faced by the Students in the Government Secondary Schools
1.	Difficulty in understanding the lessons taught by teachers in the classroom, no quality teachers and teaching, insufficient teachers, no use of teaching aids by teachers, unclean handwriting, incomplete syllabus, irregularity and absenteeism among teachers, bad teaching style and methods, classroom management problem etc. Inability of Head of institution in managing and controlling the school.
2.	No transportation service, separate toilet rooms, safe water drinking facility, proper playground, canteen, assembly hall etc.
3.	No electricity, computer and internet connectivity, No music,Yoga and NCC teachers

4.	Absence of library, good books and laboratory and scope for experimentation
6.	Unclean classroom, students' disobedience, No strict rules and regulations
7.	No facilities for games and sports and any physical support for co-curricular activities, No career counseling cell

Interpretation: The main problems faced by the government secondary school students include shortage of subject teachers, particularly Mathematics and Science, difficulty in understanding the lessons taught by teachers in the classroom, lack of quality teachers, incomplete syllabus, irregularity and absenteeism among teachers, bad teaching style and methods, having no access to basic infrastructure facilities such as drinking water, separate toilets for boys and girls, proper conduction of co-curricular activities, absence of Science laboratory, library, computers, sport opportunity, lack of vocational courses, etc.

Generally, both in government and private secondary schools, teachers use traditional method of teaching and there is a problem relating to incomplete syllabus by the teachers. In such situations and circumstances, it becomes impossible to expect creativity and innovative ideas from the students as well as overall development. Therefore, the educational aim of Gandhiji on 'All Round Development' fails to meet its goal. Children studying under such conditions would not yield good performance and even though they perform well and achieve good academic performance in the academic years. There is a possibility that they will be unable to compete the outside world after passing out of these schools in terms of knowledge, skills, and innovative outcome. Besides, they may lack confidence for Higher Education. It is evident that in the state of Arunachal Pradesh, many students end up their education in lower job markets and get self employed after reaching the secondary level of education in order to earn their livelihood. Especially for the students who come from low socio-economic background, their only expectation is the government schools, whatever skills they receive, they expect to receive from the government schools only.

But unfortunately, due to the presence of the above problems, these students are left undeveloped.

The pass percentage of students in the secondary schools run by the government from the past to the present years have shown that government schools are lacking behind the private schools in academic performance. From the U-DISE source it came to light that the average pass percentage of 10th grade students in the government secondary schools during the academic years 2013-2017 mostly falls between 50% to 70%, whereas that of private secondary school students falls between 90% to 100%. Therefore, there are many things to consider for the achievement of secondary schools and the students.

Whereas, the most severe problems faced by the students of private secondary schools include frequent change of teachers, inexperienced teachers, and pressure of high competition. Although, they face such problems, yet they enjoy better facilities, better quality of education, effective teachers, opportunity to use ICTs, enjoy variety of co-curricular activities, discipline, better communication, strict regulation and routine, teachers' regularity, obedience and sincerity, teachers' using teaching aids, transportation facility, better drinking water facility, scope for creativity, and so on compare to the government secondary school students. Besides, these students have access to exposure trips, educational tour, field trips, and excursion. These are some of the positive factors which enhance not only the intellectual growth but overall development of the students. The evidence can be viewed from the secondary education sources of the state as the sources reveal that the secondary school students of private management scored much higher than the government secondary school students in terms of academic achievement year by year. Looking at the examination result of AISSE, 2017, we find that 18835 students from government secondary schools appeared in the examination, out of which 12107 passed, i.e., pass percentage was 64.27%, whereas from the private secondary schools, 6057 appeared in the examination, out of which 5224 passed, i.e., pass percentage was 86.24%. Thus, the performance of private secondary schools is much better than that of government secondary schools.

Objective VIII. *To study the Attitude of Secondary School Students in Arunachal Pradesh towards Secondary Education with regard to management.*

Here, the attitude of secondary school students towards the secondary education is being studied using Likert's five point scale. Also, the significant difference will be tested between the attitude of government and private secondary school students towards secondary education in Arunachal Pradesh.

Interpretation: The responses made by the secondary school students reveal that their attitude regarding the secondary education is high. It also indicates that the secondary school students are positive towards the secondary education. Most of the students believe that secondary education solely depends on the quality of primary education, but their responses also reveal that most of them are unable to decide whether secondary education needs a separate institutional plan for its progress.

Regarding evaluation pattern, the students believe that removal of CCE pattern of evaluation is beneficial, and the reason for its failure is due to inability to evaluate students' real learning. They favour more to marking system over grading system of evaluation and mostly believe that the examination and evaluation are transparent and unbiased in schools.

Secondary education having no scope for vocational education and whether secondary education in Arunachal Pradesh is preparing learners for future employment in the statements 18 and 27 are responded undecided by most of the students. But, to both the negative statements (11 and 19) which state that secondary education does not provide base for scientific studies and activities, and there is least importance given for creative thinking ability, most of the students either responded disagree or strongly disagree. This explains their positive attitude towards the secondary education.

Hypothesis 1: There exists no significant difference in the Attitude of Secondary School Students in Arunachal Pradesh towards Secondary Education with regard to management.

Table 3.28: Summary of the computed scores for the Attitude of Government and Private Secondary School Students towards Secondary Education.

Attitude of Secondary School Students of Arunachal Pradesh towards Secondary Education with respect to Management Variable							
Management	N	Mean	S.D.	df	Calculated t – Value	Table Value	Remarks
Govt.	1213	94.07	10.98	2081	0.935	1.96 (0.05 level) & 2.58 (0.01 level)	Not Significant at 0.05 & 0.01 levels of Confidence
Private	870	95.14	10.56				

Interpretation: With the above computed scores it came to light that the calculated t-value 0.935 is less than the table values 1.96 at 0.05 level and 2.58 at 0.01 level of confidence. Therefore, the null hypothesis is accepted. In the light of this, it can be concluded that there exists no significant difference in the attitude of government and private secondary school students of Arunachal Pradesh towards Secondary Education with respect to Management variable. The difference in the mean scores between the two is not significant, but the attitude of students in private secondary schools is little higher than that of government secondary school students of Arunachal Pradesh with the mean score difference of 1.07.

Objective IX: *To find out the Functions of Secondary Education from the State Government Officials of Arunachal Pradesh.*

For this objective, the Government Education Officers of Arunachal Pradesh were interviewed. The interviews were basically conducted for finding out the Functions of Secondary Education in state. The findings are presented below.

Table 3.29: Responses of the Government Education Officers of Arunachal Pradesh on the Problems of Secondary Education

Sl. No.	Items/ Questions	Responses		
1.	Which are the Programmes that are not functioning well, as per the secondary education policy in Arunachal Pradesh?	i) Vocational Education ii) Science inspired Award MANAV iii) Girls' incentives iv) IEDSS		
2.	What are the problems regarding teacher posting?	i) Political involvement, ii) Medical ground iii) No proper rule regarding teacher posting iv) Terrain, criss-cross road or topography of the posting place		
3.	Are there any rules for posting duration?	i) There is no rule ii) Every 3 years iii) RMSA- non transferable and state govt.- as per Commission		
4.	What are the ratios for each secondary school?	i) 1:40 ii) 1:30		
5.	Does the authority face Hindrance/ political pressure at the time of teacher recruitment?	Yes	10	66.66%
		No	5	33.33%
6.	Where does the problem lie while selecting quality/skilled teachers?	i) Political pressure ii) Corruption iii) Untrained teachers iv) Restriction on the selection of non-APST teachers particularly in Science and Maths subjects		

7.	What are the actions taken by the state authority against absentee teachers?	i) State authority issue show cause notice to all absentee teachers ii) Suspend and terminate in case of contractual teachers iii) Hold up Pay and allowance
8.	Suggest some steps to stop backdoor entry during teacher recruitment in Arunachal Pradesh.	i) Total number of vacant posts are to be recorded every month by investigating retired teachers ii) Recruitment responsibility should be shifted to Arunachal Pradesh Public Service Commission iii) Mass recruitment for whole state to be conducted once in a year iv) Only candidate who cleared APTET/CTET to be allowed
9.	Share some points on provision to stop school boundary land encroachment.	i) Serving eviction order and Lodge FIR ii) Take help from public and administration team, Gram Panchayat, local people. iii) fund available to construct boundary wal iv) District authority under DC conduct survey in existing secondary schools to perceive status of school campus and check campus encroachment.
10.	There are some defunct schools in the state observed after the declaration of CBSE results. Share how do you take up this matter.	i) Defunct school may shut down and teachers of these schools to be shifted to schools where teachers are required ii) Up graded to residential schools with posting of regular Headmaster iii) Identify the reasons and take important steps for functioning of the particular school.
11.	Share some points on the problems of secondary education in Arunachal Pradesh.	i) no quality education and irregular classes ii) mismanagement of funds iii) No laboratory and its equipments iv) Many schools are functioning without Headmaster v) Insufficient teachers and absence of subject teachers especially Mathematics and Science vi) Overcrowded students vii) Lack of teacher quarters, electricity, computers, and school boundary wall. viii) Irregularity among teachers as well as students and no punishment for absenteeism among them

Interpretation: The above table reveals the responses of the government education officers of Arunachal Pradesh regarding the problems of secondary education. The following are the systematic interpretation of their responses.

- Programmes such as Vocational Education, Science inspired Award MANAV, Girls' incentives, and IEDSS are not functioning as per expectation of secondary education policy in Arunachal Pradesh.
- There are various problems relating to teacher's posting such as political involvement, medical ground, lack of proper rule regarding teacher's posting, criss-cross road or topography of the posting place, etc.
- Regarding posting duration of the teachers, the education officers indicated that, there is no rule but some responded that posting duration is of three years with the condition that teachers under RMSA are not transferable and transfer of state government teacher is determined by the Commission.
- There was a variation in understanding the teacher-student ratio for secondary schools, as some indicated that it should be 1:40 and for some other, it should be 1:30.
- To a question relating to whether the authority face hindrance/political pressure at the time of teacher recruitment, 66.66% of these officers responded 'Yes' and the remaining 33.33% 'No'. This shows that authorities mostly face hindrance and political pressure during recruitment of teachers.
- According to officers, the problems lie while selecting quality/skilled teachers in political pressure, corruption, untrained teachers, and restriction on the selection of non-APST teachers, particularly in Science and Maths subjects.
- The state authority takes action against absentee teachers in various ways which include issuance of show cause notice to all absentee teachers, suspension

and termination in case of contractual teachers, holding up of pay and allowances, issuance of warning letter, etc.

- Steps suggested by the education officers to stop backdoor entry during the recruitment of teachers in Arunachal Pradesh are: total number of vacant posts are to be recorded every month by investigating the number of retired teachers, recruitment responsibility should be given to Arunachal Pradesh Public Service Commission, mass recruitment for whole state to be conducted once in a year, only candidate who have cleared APTET/CTET to be allowed, etc.
- Some of the points suggested by education officers on the provision to stop encroachment of school boundary land are: serving eviction order and lodging of FIR against the encroachers; taking help from local public, administration, gram panchayat; making fund available for constructing boundary wall; and conducting survey by the district authority under DC in existing secondary schools to perceive status of school campus and extent of encroachment.
- Regarding defunct schools in Arunachal Pradesh which were observed after the declaration of CBSE results, the officers suggested that defunct schools should be shut down and teachers of these schools should be shifted to schools where teachers are required; these schools should be degraded to upper primary schools and proper care and assistance should be given to such schools for up gradation; these schools should be up graded to residential schools with posting of regular Headmasters and reasons for the defunct should be found out and important steps should be taken for functioning of the particular school.
- Some of the important problems of secondary education were indicated by these officers which include: no quality education and irregular classes; mismanagement of funds; no laboratory or laboratory

with no equipments; schools without Headmasters; insufficient teachers and absence of subject teachers especially Mathematics and Science; overcrowded classrooms; lack of quarters for teachers, electricity, and school boundary wall; and irregularity among teachers as well as students and no punishment for absenteeism among them.

Table 3.30: Response of the Government Education Officers of Arunachal Pradesh on the Development of Secondary Education.

Sl. No.	Items/Questions	Response	F	%
1.	Is RMSA programme functioning as per the policy guidelines in Arunachal Pradesh?	Yes	14	93.33%
		No	1	6.66%
2.	Share some of the state policy programmes which are effectively implemented for the quality enhancement of the secondary education.	i) CMSSY ii) Vidya scheme, incentives to girls' education iii) IEDSS iv) SSA, RMSA, Samagra Shiksha Abhiya		
3.	Are you satisfied with the existing infrastructure facilities in the schools of Arunachal Pradesh?	Yes	5	33.33%
		No	10	66.66%

4.	Indicate the status and feasibility of infrastructure facilities provided to the schools by the state government. a) Buildings/Rooms b) Furniture c) Classroom/ Blackboard/Fans d) Laboratory Room e) Library with books f) Sport items g) Computer room and teachers	a) Adequate	Inadequate	4	11	26.66%	73.33%
		b) Adequate	Inadequate	6	9	40%	60%
		c) Adequate	Inadequate	5	10	33.33%	66.66%
		d) Adequate	Inadequate	5	10	33.33%	66.66%
		e) Adequate	Inadequate	3	12	20%	80%
		f) Adequate	Inadequate	3	12	20%	80%
		g) Adequate	Inadequate	4	11	26.66%	73.33%
5.	Do you have separate grievance redrehssal cell for the secondary education in the state?	Yes		2		13.33%	
		No		13		86.66%	
6.	Is the release of funds to the institution in the state satisfactory?	Yes		6		40%	
		No		9		60%	
7.	Are the funds utilized properly?	Yes		9		60%	
		No		6		40%	
8.	How often does your department organize inspection visits to the secondary schools?	i) Whenever required ii) Once in a month iii) Yearly district-wise iv) Not regular					
9.	Who are the team committee members of the inspection team?	i) DDSE, Block Education Officer (BEO), BRCC, CRCC, DSE, CO, DC etc ii) Local administration officers					
10.	Does your department provide scholarship to the students?	Yes		14		93.33%	
		No		1		6.66%	
11.	What are the scholarships provided to the students by your department?	i) Merit scholarship		12		80%	
		ii) ST/SC scholarship		7		46.66%	
		iii) Any other		4		26.66%	

12.	Are you satisfied with the present performance/result of the secondary schools?	Yes	3	20%
		No	12	80%
13.	Does the state government keep records of the private schools in Arunachal Pradesh?	Yes	15	100%
		No	0	0%
14.	Is there any provision for vocational education in secondary schools of the state?	Yes	2	13.33%
		No	13	86.66%
15.	Suggest some ways to improve the present education system.	i) subject teachers are to be posted in every school with headmaster		
		ii) Transference in fund		
		iii) All teachers should complete the given syllabus and go for revision		
		iv) Teachers should be accommodated in school campus, student-teacher ratio should be maintained,		
		v) stop involvement of money power and political interference		
		vi) Compulsory entrance exam conducted to select students for admission		
		vii) Career Counselling Cell to be opened.		

Interpretation: The above table reveals the responses of the government education officers of Arunachal Pradesh regarding the development of secondary education in the state. The following are systematic interpretation of their responses.

- 93.33% of the education officers believe that RMSA programme in the state is functioning as per the policy guidelines of the government.
- According to education officers, state policy programmes such as CMSSY, Vidya Scheme, incentives to girls' education, IEDSS, SSA, RMSA, etc. have been effectively implemented for the quality enhancement of the secondary education.
- Most of these officers (66.66%) are not satisfied with the existing infrastructure facilities in the schools of Arunachal Pradesh except for the few (33.33%).

- Most of the education officers are not satisfied with the status and feasibility of infrastructure facilities provided to the secondary schools by the state government. 73.33% of the education officers believe that buildings/rooms are inadequate in secondary schools, 60% believe that furniture are inadequate, 66.66% believe that classrooms, blackboards, and fans are not adequate in the schools, 66.66% believe that laboratory rooms are inadequate, 80% believe that library and sport facilities are not adequate, and 73.33% believe that computer room and computer teacher are not adequate in these schools.
- 86.66% of the education officers accepted that they do not have separate grievance readdressal cell for the secondary education in the state.
- 60% of the education officers accepted that the release of funds to the institution in the state is not satisfactory, but they believe that funds are utilized properly.
- Education officers have varied views regarding the inspection of schools. Some said that the department organizes inspection whenever required, according to some once in a month, according to some other yearly district-wise, and some of them indicated that it is not regular.
- The inspection team has members from DDSE, BEO, BRCC, CRCC, DSE, CO, DC, and local administration officers.
- Most of the education officers (99.33%) accepted that the department provides scholarship to the students.
- 80% of the education officers are not satisfied with the present performance of the secondary schools.
- All the education officers accepted that the state government keeps the records of the private schools in the state.
- Most of the education officers (86.66%) accepted that there is no provision for Vocational Education in the secondary schools of the state.

- The suggestions of the officers for the improvement of the secondary education in the state include: posting of required number of subject teachers and regular Headmaster in every school; textbooks to be sent in advance and admission to be done on time; on time transfer of funds; on time completion of syllabus and revisions; in campus accommodation of teachers; student-teacher ratio to be maintained; teacher-training should be conducted time to time; stopping the involvement of money power and political interference in the school matters; compulsory entrance exam for admission in the schools; opening of career counselling cell in each school; and regularity of teachers required and should be encouraged.

Conclusion

The analysis and interpretation have been done in a systematic manner with the help of some figures and tables. In order to fulfil the objectives, first of all the development of Secondary Education in Arunachal Pradesh from 1947 to 2017 was examined. After which the investigation was carried out on the enrolment, retention, and dropout rate of 10th grade students of Arunachal Pradesh. It was followed by writing of the administrative set up for the functioning of secondary schools, investigation of the availability of infrastructure facilities, and academic achievement of 10th grade students. One of the important objectives in this study was to find out the problems faced by the Principals/Headmasters, Teachers, and Students at secondary education level. It was, therefore, investigated and presented accordingly. Apart from this, the attitude of students regarding Secondary Education was examined. Finally, the responses of the government education officers regarding development and problems of secondary education were recorded and added to this chapter.

4

Summary and Conclusion

Introduction

Education is an important part of an individual's life as it enables him/her to gain the skills required to face the varied situations in life. It is very important that every person should gain the right education for his/her overall development. In the process of gaining the right education, secondary education is the most important junction from where every student has to pass to gain entry in the higher education.

The level of growth and development of a nation is gauged by examining the moral, intellectual, and professional status of its younger generation. The future of a country depends on its youths whose development depends on the system of education that is prevalent in the country. In turn, the competence of such a system and all the institutions that may be found therein may be further ascertained from taking a look at problems that may hinder its efficiency in various areas and to varying extents. Every educational institution has to be administered on systematic lines so as to yield good results. In principle, many Government policies have been implemented for the development of secondary education but in term of practical application, the various tenets associated with them by and large neglected.

Research evidences show that secondary education is one of the fastest growing sectors in most of the countries further emphasizing the need of universalization of secondary education. Though secondary education forms an integral part in the development of the entire education system, very few studies have examined the related issues and problems of secondary education in different part of the states in our country. There exists a pressing need to enlighten government and non-government organisations to identify the crucial problems of schools and to give emphasis on proper management and administration in the context of our deteriorating educational system.

Secondary Education is a crucial stage in the educational ladder as it prepares the students for higher education as well as for job market. The way education is increasingly linked to knowledge, skills, and employment at each stage has its relative value in the development of human capital. Of late, state policies have rightly prioritized elementary education as a thrust area and have demarcated higher education for research and development. However, secondary education, that is the main link between elementary and higher education, has remained neglected not only at policy level but also in research and analysis. According to Secondary Education Commission (1953-53), "The secondary school must make itself responsible for equipping its students adequately with civic as well as vocational efficiency—and the qualities of character that go with it—so that they may be able to play their part worthy and competently in the improvement of national life". Thus, the quality of secondary education also determines the progress, development, and quality of higher education. Therefore, it is important to connect secondary education with skill development and essential to strengthen this stage by providing greater access and also by improving quality education in a significant way.

Since independence there has been considerable expansion of secondary education. Following the Mudaliar Commission Report (1952), efforts have been made to revamp the secondary school system though without much success. The National Education Commission (1964-66), popularly known as Kothari Commission, made several recommendations to improve the quality, content, and methodology of secondary education. The National Education Policy (1968) pleaded for extended secondary education facilities to areas and classes which had been denied these in the past. The policy attempted to relate education to work and employment by introducing 'Socially

Useful Productive Work (SUPW) and emphasized vocational education and technical education as components of secondary education. However, it still remains an unfulfilled goal due to non-functional vocational course, practically lacking trained teachers, absence of proper linkages with the job market, and treatment of vocational stream as inferior by both students and parents in our society. In this perspective, Secondary Education is considered as midway to higher learning, and the importance of it is being realized in the present scenario of world economy.

Mission Objectives of Secondary Education

The vision for secondary education is to make good quality education available, accessible, and affordable to all young persons in the age group of 14 to 18 years. With this vision in mind the following are to be achieved:

achieved:

- To provide a secondary school within a reasonable distance of any habitation—within 5 kilometres for a secondary school and 7–10 kilometres for a higher secondary school.
- To ensure universal access of secondary education along with universal retention.
- To provide access to secondary education with special reference to economically weaker section of the society, the girls, children with special needs, and other marginalized categories like SC, ST, OBC, and EBM (Educationally Backward Minorities).

The Draft National Education Policy (2019): Drawing inputs from the T.S.R. Subramanian Committee report and the Ministry of Human Resource Development (MHRD), the K. Kasturirangan Committee has produced the policy document aiming to universalize the pre-primary education by 2025 and provide foundational literacy/numeracy for all by 2025. Now, the policy document is out in the public domain for discussion and comments. The policy aims at making India a knowledge superpower by equipping students with the necessary skills and knowledge. It also focuses on eliminating the shortage of manpower in Science and Technology, academics, and industry. The draft policy is built on foundational pillars of Access, Equity, Quality, Affordability, and Accountability.

Many commissions and committees have given their views on structure and functioning of Secondary Education in India right from Secondary Education Commission 1952 till NPE 1986. But, many changes have undergone in the society of 21st century. In this context, Secondary Education has also to address the changes taking place in the society in its curriculum and objectives.

Educational Scenario in Arunachal Pradesh

Arunachal Pradesh, the land of rising Sun, is located in the North-Eastern part of the Indian Territory. It is a beautiful state in the North-Eastern lower Himalaya. It is the 24th state of India which spreads over an area of 84000 sq. km. It is situated between 26.28° N and 29.33° N latitude and 91.20° E and 97.30° E longitude. It has a long international border with China to the North and North-East, Myanmar to the East, and Bhutan to the West. It is the largest state in area in the Northeast region. The literacy rate of the state as per 2011 census report is 54.74 percent out of which 64.07 percent are male and 44.27 percent are female. Most of the population in Arunachal Pradesh is comprised of tribal people. There are major 25 tribes living peacefully in different parts of the state. They have their own life style, customs, traditions, culture, folk songs, stories, etc.

According to 2011 census, the highest literacy rate in the state was in Lower Subansiri district (74.3 percent) and the lowest was in Kurung Kumey district (48.8 percent). As per U-DISE, in 2014-15, the literacy rate in the state was 65.38 percent and the state possessed 415 secondary schools with 53.67 percent enrolment. The gross access ratio at the state level was 52.74 percent which was lower than the national average of 71.46 percent.

The spread of education has brought many changes in the life styles, habits, and developmental aspects of Arunachal Pradesh. At the beginning of 20th century, the condition of the education system in Arunachal Pradesh was absolutely in traumatic condition. The literacy rate in Arunachal Pradesh was below 1 percent in 1947. There were no schools in this region. The first school in the region was set up in 1918 at Pasighat in East Siang. During 1952-52 there were only 67 lower primary schools and only one middle school in the whole region.

Earlier this *'Land of Dawn lit mountains'* was commonly known as North East Frontier Agency (NEFA). On 21st January 1972, it became the union territory and later on 20th February 1987, it attained the status of a complete state. However, with the attainment of the status of statehood in 1987, the progress and development in the state accelerated gradually. According to the educational statistics 2009-10 of Directorate of School Education, Arunachal Pradesh, there were 118 higher secondary schools, 195 secondary schools, 873 upper primary schools, and 1842 primary schools in the entire state. The status of recognised educational institutions increased to 139 higher secondary schools, 228 secondary schools, 1122 upper primary schools, and 2228 primary schools as per educational statistics 2014-15 of Government of Arunachal Pradesh. At present, the number of educational institutions is quite remarkable.

Background of Rashtriya Madhyamik Shiksha Abhiyan (RMSA)

The RMSA was launched in March, 2009 by the Government of India with an objective to enhance access to secondary education and improve its quality. The scheme envisages to enhance the enrolment at secondary stage by providing a secondary school within reasonable distance of every habitant. The other objectives include improving quality of education imparted at secondary level by making all secondary schools conform to prescribed norms, removing gender, socio-economic and disability barriers, and providing universal access to secondary level education.

In order to meet the challenges of Universalisation of Secondary Education (USE), there is a need of a paradigm shift in the conceptual design of secondary education. The guiding principles in this regard are: Universal Access, Equality and

Social Justice, Relevance and Development, and Curricular and Structural Aspects. Universalisation of secondary education gives opportunity to move towards equality. The concept of 'common school' will be encouraged. If these values are to be established in the system, all types of schools including unaided private schools have to contribute towards Universalisation of Secondary Education (USE) by ensuring adequate enrolment for the children from under privileged society and Below Poverty Line (BPL) families.

Goals and Objectives of RMSA

1. To ensure that all secondary schools have physical facilities, staff, and supplies according to the prescribed standard in the RMSA norms with special emphasis on achieving and sustaining a pupil/teacher ratio of 30, pupil/classroom ratio of 40, adequate and fully equipped laboratories, computer rooms, and libraries.
2. To provide full financial support in case of Government, Local Body, and Government aided schools; and also encourage Public Private Partnership (PPP) of various kinds and extent with NGOs and private providers of education.
3. To improve access to secondary schooling to all children according to norms—through proximate location of secondary schools within 5 kms and higher secondary within 7 to 10 kms; and safe transport arrangements/ residential facilities, depending on local circumstances.
4. To ensure that no child is deprived of secondary education of satisfactory quality due to poverty, gender, socio-economic, disability, and other barriers.
5. To improve quality of secondary education through appropriate curriculum development, learning methodology, and teachers' training.

Achievement of the above goals and objectives would also, inter alia signify substantial progress in the direction of the Common School System.

Samagra Shiksha Abhiyan (SSA)/Integrated Scheme of School Education (ISSE) in Arunachal Pradesh

Samagra Shiksha Abhiyan started in Arunachal Pradesh on 1st April 2018 with a vision to ensure inclusive and equitable quality education from Pre-school to Senior Secondary stage in accordance with the Sustainable Development Goal (SDG) for Education. The primary objectives of this scheme are, by 2030, to ensure all boys and girls complete free, equitable, and quality primary and secondary education leading to relevant and effective learning outcomes, and to eliminate gender disparities in education and ensure equal access to all levels of education and vocational training for the vulnerable, including persons with disabilities, indigenous people, and children in vulnerable situations. This scheme focuses on two more areas—teacher and use of technology for delivery of quality education.

The major components of Samagra Shiksha Abhiyan are: Universal Access including infrastructure development and retention; RTE entitlements including uniforms, textbooks, etc.; community mobilization; innovations; gender and equity; and pre-primary education and vocational education.

Achievements under SSA in Arunachal Pradesh include opening of 81 secondary schools, functioning of 400 bedded hostels at secondary level schools, 5758 additional classrooms, 2106 boys and 3280 girls toilets, 315 toilets for Children with Special Needs, drinking water facilities in 1874 schools, boundary walls in 1068 schools, electricity in 626 schools, ramps in 869 schools, 172 computer rooms, 154 library rooms, 200 bedded girls hostel, and 151 science laboratories in 229 secondary and higher secondary schools.

Rational of the Study

Secondary education plays a crucial role in the formal schooling system as it has been regarded as a gateway for higher education and also a link to the job market. Since secondary education along with elementary is the backbone of every nation's education system, to make this stage of education successful and relevant to the society, there is need to provide quality education at this stage, which will make balance between continued learning and the world of work. The key elements on which the quality education depends are student's performance, teacher's performance, evaluation procedures, adherence to time frames, and infrastructure supports in achieving the set goals.

The present study intends to provide a comprehensive picture on the development and problems of secondary education. It is felt that in spite of its great value for the development process as per the secondary education policies and schemes, the performance of secondary education has been far from satisfactory in its implementation. Like in any other state, the system of education in Arunachal Pradesh is also based on education policy of the nation. However, some variations are still being found in the educational structure within the school level. Sarva Shiksha Abhiyan and Rashtriya Madhyamik Shiksha Abhiyan (RMSA) have been launched in the State of Arunachal Pradesh in the year 2001 and 2010, respectively. Secondary Education in Arunachal Pradesh has lots of shortcomings. The dropout rate is alarming at the secondary level—Tirap district has the highest dropout rate of 12.65% and Upper Siang of 10.7%, which requires special attention and intervention. The gross Access Ratio at the state level is 52.74% which is lower than the national average of 71.46%. Since last few years the state has not reported the conduction of in-service training for the teachers. Under IEDSS, no special educator has been recruited in the state due to lack of availability of qualified special educators as per the scheme. There is lack of adequate number of trained teachers who are the actual disseminators of knowledge. Recent appointments of teachers under SSA are made on ad-hoc basis who are mostly not dedicated and remain absent at the posted schools due to delayed disbursement of their salary, lack of quarter accommodations, etc. Such untrained and unmotivated teachers truly cannot provide quality education to students who require a strong foundation of knowledge. Most of the secondary schools in the interior rural areas do not have electricity connection which prevents teachers from using modern devices like computer for teaching and management of schools. In the 21st century, lack of infrastructure is a source of challenge and will not let the schools as well as the education system grow to its fullest potential which is the matter of great concern.

The introduction of Continuous Comprehensive Evaluation (CCE) scheme in all the government schools in 2010 has caused a major setback in the quality of education in Arunachal Pradesh. It is observed that none of the stakeholders have understood the concept of CCE. Till 2017 session the students were awarded grades and promoted without continuous observation and assessment which has affected the quality of education as well as the products of the system.

Therefore, it is imperative to explore the problems of Secondary Education in order to come out with such discussions that will provide light to future policy makers and state educational authorities to facilitate or inhibit the performance of secondary education system in the state. For this, the investigator has taken appropriate steps to conduct a thorough study on the development and problems of Secondary Education in Arunachal Pradesh.

Statement of the Problem: To study the development and problems of Secondary Education in the state of Arunachal Pradesh.

Objectives of the Study

(i) To examine the Development of Secondary Education in the state of Arunachal Pradesh from 1947 to 2017.

(ii) To investigate the Enrolment, Promotion, Repetition, and Dropout rates of Students at the Secondary Stage of selected districts.

(iii) To explore the administrative set up for the functioning of Secondary Education.

(iv) To investigate the availability of infrastructure facilities in Secondary Schools.

(v) To examine the academic achievement of Secondary School Students of Arunachal Pradesh.

(vi) To compare academic achievements of 10th grade students of Arunachal Pradesh before and after the removal of CCE pattern of evaluation.

(vii) To find out the problems faced by Principals/ Headmasters, Teachers, and Students of Secondary Schools in Arunachal Pradesh.

(viii) To study the Attitude of Secondary School Students in Arunachal Pradesh towards Secondary Education relating to management.

(ix) To find out the Functions of Secondary Education from the State Government Officials of Arunachal Pradesh.

Research Questions

(a) How is the development of Secondary Education in Arunachal Pradesh?

(b) What is the status of Secondary School in Arunachal Pradesh?

(c) Is there satisfactory in enrolment of Secondary Schools stage?

(d) How is the administrative set up for the functioning of Secondary Education?

(e) Are the infrastructural facilities available in Secondary Schools?

(f) Is the academic performance satisfactory at secondary level?

(g) Is there academic performance difference in male and female students?

(h) How is the teaching conducted in Secondary Schools?

(i) Which medium of instruction used in Secondary Schools?

(j) What are the effects of Continuous Comprehensive Evaluation?

(k) Are the teachers trained in Secondary Schools?

(l) What are the problems of Secondary Education in the State?

(m) How is the attitude of students regarding secondary schools?

Hypothesis of the Study

The following hypothesis has been formulated according to the nature of the present study:

H01: There exists no significant difference in the Attitude between the Government and the Private Secondary School Students towards Secondary Education.

Methodology Used

Method: The present study was based on the prevailing conditions which aimed at obtaining precise and clear information regarding the current status of the development and problems of secondary education in the state. Therefore, the researcher has adopted normative survey method of descriptive studies.

Population: All the Education Officers, Headmasters/Principals, Teachers, and Students of the Secondary Schools of Government and Private management in Arunachal Pradesh.

Sample: For the representative sample of the study, the investigator adopted Stratified Random Sampling Technique. The sample included—(i) 15 Government Education Officers, (ii) 40 Headmasters/Principals, (iii) 589 secondary school teachers and, (iv) 2083 10th grade students, taken from 50 schools in the 20 selected districts of Arunachal Pradesh.

Research Tools Employed

The study has used one Interview Schedule, four self developed Questionnaires, and some Secondary Sources. The following are the tools used by the researchers for collection of the data:

Primary Sources:

(a) *Interview Schedule:*

- Interview Schedule for the Government Education Officers.

(b) *Questionnaires:*

- Problems of the Head-in-Charge of Secondary Schools in Arunachal Pradesh (2018),

- Problems of Secondary School Teachers in Arunachal Pradesh (2018),
- Problems of Secondary School Students of Arunachal Pradesh (2018), and
- Attitude Scale for Secondary School Students towards Secondary Education (2018).

Secondary Sources (U-Dise sources from School Education Office):

- Enrolment and Academic Achievement of 10th grade students,
- Number of Secondary Schools in Arunachal Pradesh (Government and Private),
- Number of Secondary School Teachers in Arunachal Pradesh (Government and Private), and
- Dropout, Repetition, and Promotion rate of the 10th grade students in Arunachal Pradesh.

Administration of Tools and Scoring

The tools consisted of one format for Interview Schedule, four self developed questionnaires, and some secondary sources. After the collection and the development/construction of the required tools, the tools were administered to 20 selected districts of the state. The interview schedule was used to collect data from 15 Government Education Officers which was done accordingly. Besides the questionnaires were used to collect data from 40 Headmasters/Principals, 589 Secondary School Teachers, and 2083 10th grade students taken from 40 Government and Private schools in the 20 selected districts of Arunachal Pradesh.

Apart from this, the secondary sources such as Enrolment and Academic Achievement of 10th grade students, Number of Secondary Schools in Arunachal Pradesh (Government and Private), Number of Secondary School Teachers in Arunachal Pradesh (Government and Private), and Dropout, Repetition, and Promotion rate of the 10th grade students in Arunachal Pradesh were collected from U-DISE which were later administered according to the requirements of the study. In continuation to this process, the collected and administered data were scored.

Analysis and Interpretation of Data

The researchers have used appropriate statistical techniques for analysis and interpretation of data according to formulated objectives and hypotheses of the study. The statistical techniques used in the present study were Percentage, Mean, Standard Deviation, and t-test.

Main Findings of the Study

Objective I: To examine the Development of Secondary Education in the State of Arunachal Pradesh from 1947 to 2017.

Findings: Arunachal Pradesh being the late starter in the field of education, the first school opened in the year 1918 at Pasighat, the state remained backward as compared to other part of Northeast Region and the second school was opened by Adi Community of Dibang Valley in 1922 at Dambuk. Thereafter, some other schools were established before 1947 at places such as Ningroo (1934), Boleng (1940), Riga (1940), Balk (1946), Yomcha (1947), Along (1947), Pasighat (1947), etc. In all these schools, the medium of instruction was Assamese during those days. It indicates that there was not much educational development before and even after the independence, and the pace of educational development was very slow. Arunachal Pradesh (NEFA) was possessing 67 Lower Primary Schools and one Middle School with 120 teachers at Lower Primary level and 6 teachers at Middle School level, and having the enrolments of 2674 and 34, respectively. In the year 1955-56, there were 152 Lower Primary Schools, 16 Middle Schools, and 3 Secondary Schools in the whole of the state, and the literacy rate was recorded below 1.0 percent. In the year 1963-64, there were 179 Lower Primary Schools, 25 Middle Schools, and 7 Secondary and Senior Secondary Schools with 359,141, and 113 teachers, and having 7200, 2267, and 1306 enrolment of students, respectively. It shows that the pace of educational development was not satisfactory in Arunachal Pradesh during the period when it was called NEFA. Arunachal Pradesh was declared a Union Territory (UT) in 1972 and with the formation of Union Territory, educational development got accelerated. All the schools were affiliated to Central Board of Secondary

Education (CBSE), New Delhi, and English was adopted as the medium of instruction. Government of Arunachal Pradesh took interest in the educational development of the state and as a result, large numbers of schools were established in the state.

Secondary level schools were established in administrative headquarters of the districts having potentially to grow rapidly into urban centres. Most of the schools in secondary level came into existence between early 1980s and 1990s because of political consideration in upgrading middle and secondary schools. As a result, secondary schools were established in rural and inaccessible areas like Nyapin, Palin, Mechuka, Tuting, Chayang-Tajo, Sagalee, Rumgong, etc. during that period. As a result, in the year 2002, there were 156 secondary level schools in rural areas of the state. During 2013-2018, there has been a growth of secondary schools in the state, which increased from 215 to 285 government secondary schools in 2018, and the number of private secondary schools has increased from 71 to 109 in the same time period. On the same line, the number of government secondary school teachers have increased from 3979 in the year 2013 to 5860 in the year 2018 and that of private secondary school teachers from 1003 in 2013 to 1743 in 2018.

Unlike the increasing numbers of schools and teachers, the U-DISE source reveals that the students' enrolment particularly of 10th grade at the secondary schools has not been increasing year by year, as 18096 students were enrolled in the government schools in 2013 and in 2018, the number of students' enrolment was only 18063. In case of government schools, the maximum number of students enrolled in the secondary schools can be seen in the year 2017. In the private schools, the year 2016 had witnessed the maximum numbers of students' enrolment at the secondary schools which was followed by the year 2018 and then 2017.

Objective II: To investigate the Enrolment, Promotion, Repetition, and Dropout rates of students at the secondary stage of selected districts.

Findings

Enrolment: During the academic sessions 2013-2017, there has been an increasing rate of enrolment among the 10th grade secondary school students except for the year 2014. In 2014, both boys and girls reflected decrease in numbers with the total enrolments of 13577. Altogether, 88541 students were enrolled in the secondary schools at 10th grade during 2013-2017.

Promotion Rate: The state had 11.75% promotion rate of secondary school students in the year 2013. In the years 2014, 2015, 2016, and 2017, the promotion rates were 49.95%, 71.76%, 82.44%, and 42.98%, respectively.

Repetition Rate: The repetition rate of secondary school students were 3.75%, 2.16%, 1.10%, 0.70%, and 0.73% for the academic sessions 2013, 2014, 2015, 2016, and 2017, respectively.

Dropout Rate: Since the implementation of CCE pattern of evaluation, the dropout rate of the students at the secondary school stage, particularly of the 10th grade students, has dropped down to 0.00% in all the districts of Arunachal Pradesh. After the removal of CCE pattern of evaluation in 2017, as per the statistical record in the education department, it is seen that there is still 0.00% dropout rate in all the districts of Arunachal Pradesh.

Objective III: To explore the administrative set up for the functioning of secondary education.

Findings: The state of Arunachal Pradesh has been divided administratively into districts, a district into sub-division/ EAC headquarters and these further into circles. In the same vein, the administration pertaining to education has also been organized at the state and district levels and down below at sub-division or circles. Presently, at state level, the organizational structure includes a Ministry, a Secretariat, and Directorates. The functions of these three bodies include policy formulation, implementation and monitoring, and supervision.

At district level there is the establishment of Deputy Director of School Education (DDSE), which functions as an implementation, monitoring, and supervision body. Below district level, there is Assistant District Education Officer (ADEO)/Adult Education Supervisor (AES) attached to either EAC Officer or CO office when there is less number of schools. The ADEOs/AESs mainly supervises the schools. Therefore, the secondary school activities are taken up by the DDSE, then the District Project Coordinators (DPCs) followed by Block Resource Centres (BRCs) and Cluster Resource Centres (CRCs) and the concerned Head of secondary schools.

The Government of Arunachal Pradesh has bifurcated the directorate of school education into two directorates on 28th October, 2010. They are Directorate of Elementary Education and Directorate of Secondary Education. But, no proper bifurcations of the directorates have been taken so far although they are functioning separately for the last two years. Therefore, stream lining of these two directorates is necessary for their smooth functioning. Earlier, DPCs had two separate administrative functions for Elementary and Secondary Schools but now both have been integrated into one post after the implementation of Samagra Shiksha. It is to be observed that there is no change in the administrative functions of the secondary education system except that the composite budget fund has been changed in the state with the merging of centrally sponsored scheme of SSA, RMSA, and Teacher Education (TE). Accordingly, the scheme has been developed and launched to form an Integrated Scheme on School Education/Samagra Shiksha from Pre-schools to Secondary schools.

Objective IV: To investigate the availability of infrastructure facilities in Government Secondary Schools.

Findings of Headmasters/Principals:

- 100% of Headmasters/Principals of government secondary schools revealed to have their own permanent school buildings.
- 55% of the structures of school buildings are of Assamese type, 45% of RCC type, and none of the schools have Kachha type buildings.
- Only 35% of Headmasters/Principals have revealed to have sufficient playground in their schools and 45%

to have school boundary walls. Besides, 75% of them claimed to have motorable road connectivity to their schools.

- 55% of Headmasters/Principals declared to have hostel facility in their schools, 45% to have sufficient furniture, and only 25% to have Ramp/Railing facility for physically challenged. Most of the schools do not have first aid facility. 45% of them declared that they do not have separate toilet facilities for both boys and girls and 70% declared to have no appropriate drinking water facilities.
- 35% of the Headmasters/Principals responded to have libraries in their schools, but most of them don't have adequate books.
- Mostly, LCD projector and computer lab are available in these schools and none of them posses tape recorder as types of audio-visual aids.
- Most of the schools do not possess laboratory facility. Schools that possess laboratories have out dated apparatus and equipments and absence of proper furniture.
- The government secondary schools have facilities such as auditorium, quarters for teachers, Principal office, Staff's room, EDUSAT/Internet connection, computer rooms, smart classrooms, and store rooms. 90% of government secondary school Headmasters/Principals accepted to have staff rooms in their schools, 60% smart classrooms, 75% Principal office, and so on.
- Except for some of the headmasters/principals, it came to know that half the government secondary schools have sufficient desk and benches, blackboard, fans, electricity, and properly ventilated classrooms as majority of them indicated insufficiency of these facilities and not in good condition.

The responses of the private secondary school Headmasters/ Principals regarding infrastructure indicated that:

- 95% of the private secondary schools have their own land and building.
- According to 90% of the Headmasters/Principals, private secondary schools have their own permanent school buildings against 10% who declared rented school buildings.
- 5% of the Headmasters/Principals accepted to have Assamese type structure of school buildings, 80% RCC type, and 15% of the schools have kachha type structure.
- 65% of the Headmasters/Principals accepted to have sufficient playground and school boundary walls. 90% of them claimed to have motorable road connectivity to their schools.
- 85% of the schools have hostel facility and sufficient furniture and only 5% to have Ramp/Railing facility for physically challenged. Mostly schools have first aid facility. Only 10% declared that they do not have separate toilet facilities for both boys and girls and 25% declared that there is no appropriate drinking water facilities.
- 65% of the Headmasters/Principals claimed that they have their own school library. 65% said that they have adequate books, 60%-equipped with furniture, 55%-journals, and 60% to have encyclopedia in the library.
- Most of the schools have computer lab and LCD projectors.
- Most of the schools (75%) possess laboratory facilities.
- The private secondary schools have facilities such as auditorium, teachers' quarter, Principal's office, staff's room, EDUSAT/Internet connection, computer room, smart classrooms, and store room. At most, 90% schools have Principal office, and 85% of the schools have staff room and store rooms.

- Except for some of the Headmasters/Principals, it came to know that the private secondary schools have sufficient desk and benches, blackboard, fans, electricity, and properly ventilated classrooms, and majority of them indicated sufficiency of these facilities.

Findings of Government Secondary School Teachers of Arunachal Pradesh relating to infrastructure facilities:

- According to most of the government secondary school teachers, there is sufficient infrastructure in staff room, but 42.31% of teachers disagree on this.
- Only 22.88% of the teachers have revealed that their schools provide laboratory facilities for science students.
- Most of the teachers do not face difficulties in using Audio-Visual aids/teaching aids in the classrooms.
- Most of the teachers revealed that they face problem due to absence of school library and Science laboratory.
- Based on the responses of 64.39% of teachers, it is clear that they do not have access to adequate drinking water facility.
- Most of the schools have separate toilet rooms for both male and female teachers.
- Only 5.01% teachers indicated to have transportation services in their schools.

Findings of Private Secondary School Teachers of Arunachal Pradesh relating to infrastructure facilities:

- Most of the teachers accepted to have sufficient infrastructure facilities in the staff room.
- 72.59% of the teachers revealed that their schools provide laboratory facilities for science students.
- Most of the teachers do not face difficulties in using audio-visual aids/teaching aids in the classrooms.
- Most of the teachers revealed that they do not face problem in the school library.

- Based on the responses of 84.81% of teachers, it is revealed that they do have access to adequate drinking water facility.
- Most of the schools have separate toilet rooms for both male and female teachers.
- 63.33% of teachers accepted to have transportation services in their schools.

Findings of Government Secondary School Students of Arunachal Pradesh relating to infrastructure facilities:

- Most of the students revealed insufficiency of desk and benches, good condition blackboard, and properly ventilated classrooms. They also revealed that their schools have fans that are not working and unavailability of electricity.
- Few students have accepted that their schools have facilities like open auditorium hall, playground, hostel facility, EDUSAT/Internet connection, computer room, and smart classrooms. But, in most of the schools, smart classrooms and computer rooms are not functional.
- Only 23.82% of the students accepted that their schools have laboratory rooms, but that too without chemicals and instruments.
- Only 17.39% of students accepted to have access to library facilities in their schools.
- Although drinking water facility falls under student welfare facility, 81.69% of the students in these schools accepted that their schools do not have adequate and safe drinking water facility.
- 38.41% of students accepted that their schools have separate toilet rooms for both boys and girls.
- Only 3.70% of students accepted to have bus/ transportation services in their schools.

Findings of Private Secondary School Students of Arunachal Pradesh relating to infrastructure facilities:

- Most of the students accepted to have sufficiency of desk and benches, good condition blackboard, working fans, availability of electricity and properly ventilated classrooms in their schools.
- Most of the students accepted to have facilities such as auditorium hall, playground, hostel facility, career counselling cell, EDUSAT/Internet connection, computer room and smart classrooms in their schools.
- 54.94% of students accepted to have laboratory facilities in their schools and 88.16% accepted to have library facilities in their schools.
- Although drinking water facility is a student welfare facility, 54.13% of the students accepted to have no access to adequate and safe drinking water facility.
- Most of the students (97.58%) accepted to have separate toilet rooms for both boys and girls in their schools.
- Only 36.32% of students accepted to have no bus/ transportation services in their schools.

Objective V: To examine the Academic Achievement of Secondary School Students of Arunachal Pradesh.

Findings: When the district-wise academic achievement of 10th grade government secondary school students was computed, it came to light that Tawang had the highest average pass percentage, followed by East Kameng and Longding districts. Whereas Kra-Daadi had the lowest average pass percentage. In most of the districts, the average pass percentage of the 10th grade students falls within the range of 70% to 80%, and in rest of the districts it was between 50% to 70%. In the case of private schools, West Kameng district had the highest average pass percentage followed by Upper Subansiri and East Kameng districts. Lower Dibang Valley has the lowest average pass percentage. In rest of the districts, the average pass percentage among 10th grade students falls above 90%. Thus, the students of private secondary schools performed better than the students of government secondary schools.

From the year-wise trend analysis, we find that the most of the 10th grade students of the secondary schools in Arunachal Pradesh scored between 41% to 60%, and the least of them scored above 80% during the academic sessions 2013 to 2018.

From the perspective of gender analysis it is observed that both boys and girls in majority scored within the range of 41% to 60% and least of them scored above 80%. The average percentage of the 10th grade secondary school students among boys was 50.02% and that of among girls was 50.48%. It reveals that girls at 10th grade performed a little better than the boys of the 10th grade in Arunachal Pradesh.

Objective VI. To compare the academic achievement of 10th grade secondary school students of Arunachal Pradesh before and after the removal of CCE pattern of evaluation.

Findings: From the obtained data, we find that before the removal of CCE pattern of evaluation, 22.57% of the 10th grade secondary school students scored below or equal to 40% in Arunachal Pradesh. 60.49% of the students scored between 41% to 60%, 13.15% of the students scored within the range of 61% to 80%, and only 3.77% of the students secured above 80% during the academic sessions 2014-15 and 2015-16. On the other hand, after the removal of CCE pattern of evaluation, 16.35% of the students secured below or equal to 40%, 58.36% of the students secured between 41% to 60%, 21.62% of the students secured within the range of 61% to 80%, and only 3.64% of the students secured above 80% during the academic sessions 2016-17 and 2017-18. Hence, before and after the removal of the CCE pattern of evaluation, the results of 10th grade secondary school students were almost same. In both the cases, most of the students secured within the range of 41% to 60%. The average marks obtained by the 10th grade students before the removal of CCE pattern of evaluation was 50.87% and after the removal of CCE pattern of evaluation was 47.99%. It shows that the 10th grade students in Arunachal Pradesh performed a little better before the removal of CCE pattern of evaluation.

Thus, due to 'No Detention' policy, the academic achievement of 10th grade students in Arunachal Pradesh was slightly higher before the removal of CCE pattern of evaluation than the removal of CCE system. It implies that CCE pattern of evaluation is not a significant factor for the academic achievement of the 10th grade students as the quality of teaching-learning was low during the CCE system. Therefore, it can be said that CCE pattern was a failure in qualitative aspect which was ignored by the sate government during the implementation of the CCE system in the state, and 'No Detention' policy is a better means for the achievement of students at secondary level.

Objective VII: To find out the problems faced by Principals/ Headmasters, Teachers, and Students at secondary schools in Arunachal Pradesh.

Findings relating to Section–A (Teacher-related problems in the government secondary schools): It indicates that

- The number of teachers in the government secondary schools was not sufficient according to 40% of the Headmasters/Principals.
- 35% of the Headmasters/Principals indicated sufficiency of the Science teachers whereas, 65% indicated insufficiency of the Science teachers.
- 70% of the Headmasters/Principals accepted that teachers in their schools are very punctual.
- 45% of the Headmasters/Principals indicated that teachers in their schools are committed to their profession.
- 40% of the Headmasters/Principals declared that teachers in their schools very often use teaching-learning materials/teaching aids.
- According to 40% of them, government secondary schools have computer and NCC/Scouts and Guides teachers, 35% declared to have sport teachers, 15% declared to have music teachers, and unfortunately none of them declared to have Yoga teachers in their schools.

The responses of the Headmasters/Principals regarding teacher-related problems in the private secondary schools:

- The number of teachers in the private secondary schools was sufficient according to 85% of the Headmasters/ Principals.
- 75% of the Headmasters/Principals indicated sufficiency of the Science teachers in their schools.
- 90% of the Headmasters/Principals accepted that teachers in their schools are very punctual.
- 85% of the Headmasters/Principals accepted that teachers in their schools are committed to their profession.
- 65% of the Headmasters/Principals accepted that teachers in their schools very often use teaching-learning materials/teaching aids while teaching.
- According to 75% of the Headmasters/Principals, their schools have computer teachers, 45% accepted to have NCC/Scouts and Guides teachers, 60% declared to have sport teachers, 30% declared to have music teachers, and only 25% of them declared that they have Yoga teachers in their schools.

Findings relating to Section–B (Curriculum, Co-curricular activities, Teaching-Learning and Evaluation):

- Based on the responses, it is clear that 40% of the Headmasters/Principals are satisfied and 60% are not satisfied with the existing curriculum as per NCFSE, 2005. Most of them (80%) believe that the existing curriculum is relevant, productive, contextual, and up-to-date. Even the syllabus of the secondary grade is relevant according to 70% of them.
- 15% of the Headmasters/Principals found hard spots in the present curriculum and only 15% faced difficulties in the implementation of RMSA scheme.
- 40% of Headmasters/Principals responded that the school faces problems in organizing co-curricular activities and 35% responded that schools take the students to the field trips and excursion.

- The most of the Headmasters/Principals are satisfied with the attendance of the students but 60% of them are not satisfied with the academic performance of the students.
- The most of the Headmasters/Principals accepted that in their schools teachers use both Hindi and English as a medium of instruction. Mother-tongue and Hindi are used by very few teachers.
- Assessment of students in the schools are mostly done on monthly basis and then quarterly proceeded by half-yearly, annually, and then weekly.
- Interestingly, none of the Headmasters/Principals supported for CCE pattern of evaluation that is most appropriate for the teacher's attainment and holistic learning of the learners. All of them supported for existing external board system of evaluation.

The responses of the Headmasters/Principals regarding curriculum, co-curricular activities, teaching-learning and evaluation-related problems in the Private Secondary schools:

- Based on the responses, it is clear that 75% of the Headmasters/Principals are satisfied and only 25% are not satisfied with the existing curriculum as per NCFSE, 2005. Most of them (70%) believe that the existing curriculum is relevant, productive, contextual, and up-to-date. Even the syllabus of the secondary grade is relevant according to 80% of them.
- Like the case of government secondary schools, none of the Headmasters/Principals found any hard spots in the present curriculum and only 5% faced difficulties in implementation of RMSA scheme.
- Only 15% of Headmasters/Principals responded that the schools face problems in organizing co-curricular activities and 65% responded that schools take the students to field trips and excursion.
- It is revealed from the responses that most of the Headmasters/Principals are satisfied with the attendance and academic performance of the students.

- Most of the Headmasters/Principals accepted that teachers in their schools use English as the medium of instruction proceeded by both Hindi and English. Mother-tongue is used by very few teachers and no teacher uses Hindi as only the medium of instruction.
- Assessment of students in the schools are mostly done in a monthly basis and then quarterly, weekly, half-yearly, proceeded by annually.
- Only 20% of the Headmasters/Principals supported for CCE pattern of evaluation. 80% of them supported for existing external board exam.

Findings relating to Section–C (Management, Finance and Supervision):

- The School Management Committee (SMC) members are supportive according to 90% of the government secondary school Headmasters/Principals.
- 75% of the Headmasters/Principals accepted that they have institutional planning.
- According to 90% of them, school accounts are audited annually.
- 45% of the Headmasters/Principals accepted to get financial assistance on time.
- Most of the Headmasters/Principals accepted that their schools hold staff meetings whenever necessary.
- Principals/Headmasters and DDSE mostly prepare the school budget annually.
- State government officials mostly visit the schools for inspection periodically.
- The government secondary schools maintained all types of records such as teachers' attendance, students' register, admission register, CRC record, staff meeting record, PTA meeting record, and store log book. At most they maintained teachers' attendance, students' register, and admission register in their schools.

The responses of the private secondary school Headmasters/ Principals:

- The School Management Committee (SMC) members are supportive according to 80% of the private secondary school Headmasters/Principals.
- 70% of the Headmasters/Principals responded that they had institutional planning.
- According to 85% of them, school accounts are audited annually.
- 55% of the Headmasters/Principals accepted to get financial assistance on time.
- Most of the Headmasters/Principals accepted that their schools hold staff meeting whenever necessary.
- The SMC and Headmasters/Principals mostly prepare the school budget annually.
- Most of the Headmasters/Principals accepted that the state government officials visit their schools for inspection periodically.
- The private secondary schools maintained all types of records such as teachers' attendance, students' register, admission register, CRC record, staff meeting record, PTA meeting record, and store log book. At most they maintained teachers' attendance, students' register, and admission register in their schools.
- Financial assistance comes to the private secondary schools from various sources but mostly from school fees.

Above all, the main problems faced by the Headmasters/ Principals in the Government Secondary Schools include late posting of subject teachers; indiscipline in the school; lack of resources such as furniture, teaching aids, school boundary, laboratory, auditorium, quarters, etc.; sanitation problem; overcrowded classrooms; lack of moral responsibility on the part of teachers; lack of clerical personnel and shortage of group D staff; improper electrical wiring; absence of proper playground; no facilities for games and sports; untimely supply of textbooks; insufficient fund by the state government; poor

SMC attendance and time management problem among SMC members; and so on.

Whereas, the problems faced by Headmasters/Principals in the Private Secondary Schools of Arunachal Pradesh include no motivation given to students; no proper supply of textbooks; no cooperation; absence of medical facility; difficulty in arrangement of teachers; lack of library, science laboratory, good furniture, etc.; no help from government both state and central; irregularity of students; and lack of interest on the part of teachers.

In consideration to the above common problems faced by the teachers in the government secondary schools, they face some acute problems in their profession. Despite drawing good salary and having a secured job, the government secondary school teachers serving in various districts of Arunachal Pradesh are dissatisfied with the posting areas particularly in the rural areas, lack of infrastructure facilities, proper and hygiene toilets, clean drinking water facilities, lack of quarters, overburden administration and additional tasks, additional periods assigned to them on non-specialized subjects, and so on.

While reflecting on the above problems of private secondary school teachers, it is observed that although they enjoy better facilities than the government secondary school teachers, yet most of the private secondary school teachers are not satisfied with their profession. The problems faced by the private secondary school teachers include heavy workload, low salary and high expectation, job insecurity, and discrimination between Government and Private school teachers. These are some of the factors which hamper overall inputs towards the progress of students' performance and in the presence of such causes of dissatisfaction among the private school teachers, overall development of school is not possible.

Findings related to Section—B (Student related Problems): Problems faced by the Government Secondary School Students include:

- 65.86% of the students are satisfied with the teaching-learning process in their schools.

- According to 62.07% of the students, teachers are sometimes punctual.
- Majority of the students responded that their teachers never use teaching-learning materials/teaching aids.
- 56.47% of the students claimed that their teachers do not complete the syllabi on time.
- At most, teachers use lecture and demonstration method of teaching in the classrooms.
- Both Hindi and English are used mostly by the teachers as medium of instruction.
- 86.89% of the students claimed that they attend the schools regularly.
- Lack of clarity in explanation is indicated to be the reason for facing difficulty in understanding the lessons taught in the classroom at most.
- Mostly students face difficulty in learning Mathematics and Science.

The responses of the Private Secondary School Students include:

- 63.67% of the students are satisfied with the teaching-learning process of their schools.
- According to 50.68% of the students, teachers are punctual.
- 65.17% of the students accepted to have computer teachers in their schools and 43.33% of the students accepted to have sport teachers in their schools.
- Majority of the students (60.11%) responded that their teachers rarely use teaching-learning materials/teaching aids.
- 61.14% of the students claimed that their teachers complete the syllabi on time.
- At most, teachers use lecture and demonstration method of teaching in the classrooms.
- Both Hindi and English are used mostly by the teachers as medium of instruction.

- 90.11% of the students claimed that they attend the schools regularly.
- Lack of clarity in explanation is indicated to be the reason for facing difficulty in understanding the lessons taught in the classroom at most.
- Most of the students face difficulties in learning Mathematics and Science.

Findings relating to Section–C (Co-curricular Activities): Out of the 18 co-curricular activities, the government secondary schools organize dancing (78.07%) and football (75.68%) and singing at the most, whereas the students get least opportunities in activities such as table tennis (1.23%), basketball (2.80%), mime play (4.36%), instrumental (6.26%), exhibition (14.01%), debate (25.96%), badminton (23.49%), cricket (18.54%), and seminars (42.12%) in their schools. It reflects that most of the government secondary schools are not encouraging co-curricular activities due to shortage of proper playgrounds, lack of physical sport teachers, and not organizing recreation activities for all round development of the students at this stage.

Whereas, the private secondary schools organize dancing (97.58%) and singing (92.06%), drawing and painting (91.60%), quiz (81.37%), seminar (61.60%), debate (62.06%), and extempore speech (85.63%) at the most. And at the least they have table tennis (12.98%) and mime play (19.08%) in their schools. Thus, the private secondary schools organize all most of the co-curricular activities.

Findings relating to Section–D (Others):

- 79.63% of the students accepted that their schools have implemented the "Swachh Bharat Abhiyan".
- Some of the students revealed that their schools create social discrimination atmosphere.
- Majority of the students do not believe that their school pressurizes them to play or sit with the same gender only.
- Majority of the student consider that their syllabus at secondary grade is relevant to the present context.

- Most of the students consider existing external board exam pattern to be most appropriate.

Whereas, regarding the private secondary school students, we get:

- 79.88% of the students accepted that their schools have implemented the "Swachh Bharat Abhiyan".
- Majority of the students do not believe that their school pressurizes them to play or sit with the same gender only.
- Majority of the students consider that their syllabus at secondary grade is relevant to the present context.
- 53.10% of the students consider existing external board exam pattern to be most appropriate.

The main problems faced by the students at the secondary school stage include shortage of subject teachers particularly Mathematics and Science; difficulty in understanding the lessons taught by teachers in the classroom; no quality teachers; incomplete syllabus; irregularity and absenteeism among teachers; bad teaching style and methods; having no access to basic infrastructure facilities such as drinking water, separate toilets for boys and girls; lack in the proper conduction of co-curricular activities; absenteeism among teachers; absence of Science laboratory, library, computers, and sport opportunity; lack of Vocational courses; etc. Generally, both in government and private secondary schools, teachers use traditional method of teaching and there is a problem relating to incomplete syllabus by the teachers.

In such situations and circumstances, it becomes impossible to expect creativity and innovative ideas from the students as well as overall development. Therefore, the educational aim of Gandhiji on 'All Round Development' fails to meet its goal. Children studying under such conditions would not yield good performance and even though they perform well and achieve good academic performance in the academic years of these schools, there is a possibility that they will be unable to compete the outside world after passing out from these schools in terms of knowledge, skills, and innovative outcome. Besides, they may lack confidence for Higher Education. It is evident that in the state of Arunachal Pradesh, many students end up their education in lower job markets and get self employed after reaching the secondary level of education in order to earn their livelihood. Especially for the students who come from low socio-economic background, their only expectation is the government schools, whatever skills they receive, they expect to receive from the government schools only. But unfortunately, due to the presence of the above problems, these students are left undeveloped.

The pass percentages of students in the secondary schools run by the government from the past to the present years have shown that government schools are lacking behind the private schools in academic performance. From the U-DISE source it came to light that the average pass percentage of 10th grade students in the government secondary schools during the academic years 2013 to 2017 mostly falls between 50% to 70% whereas, the private secondary school students have their average pass percentage mostly falling between 90% to 100%. Therefore, there are many things to reconsider for the achievement of secondary schools and the students.

Whereas, the most severe problems faced by students of private secondary schools include frequent change of teachers, inexperienced teachers, and pressure of high competition. Although they face such problems, they enjoy better facilities, better quality education, effective teachers, opportunity to use ICT, variety of co-curricular activities, discipline, better communication, strict regulation and routine, teachers' regularity, obedience and sincerity, teachers' using teaching aids, transportation facility, better drinking water facility, scope for creativity, and so on compare to the government secondary school students. Besides, these students have access to exposure trips, educational tour, field trips, and excursion. These are some of the positive factors which enhance not only the intellectual growth but overall development of the students. The evidence can be viewed from the secondary education sources of the state as the sources reveal that the secondary school students of private management scored much higher than the government secondary school students in terms of academic achievement year by year. Thus, private secondary schools are great boon to our state in terms of secondary education.

Objective VIII. To study the Attitude of Secondary School Students in Arunachal Pradesh towards Secondary Education with regard to management.

Findings: The Likert's five point scale was applied while describing the attitude of students regarding secondary education. And the significant difference was tested between the attitude of government and private secondary school students towards secondary education in Arunachal Pradesh.

The responses made by the secondary school students revealed that their attitude regarding the secondary education is high. It also indicates that the secondary school students are positive towards the secondary education. According to the responses on the statements by students revealed that mostly students believed that secondary education solely depends on quality primary education but their responses also revealed that most of them are unable to decide whether secondary education needs a separate institutional plan for its progress.

With respect to evaluation pattern, the students believe that removal of CCE pattern of evaluation is beneficial and the reason for its failure is due to inability to evaluate students' real learning. They favour more to marking system over grading system of evaluation and mostly believe that the examination and evaluation are transparent and unbiased in schools.

Secondary education having no scope for Vocational education and whether secondary education in Arunachal Pradesh is preparing learners for future employment in the statements 18 and 27 are responded undecided by most of the students. But, to both the negative statements (11 and 19) which states that secondary education does not provide base for scientific studies and activities and there is least importance given for creative thinking ability, most of the students either responded disagree or strongly disagree. This explains their positive attitude towards the secondary education.

Hypothesis 1: There exists no significant difference in the Attitude of Secondary School Students in Arunachal Pradesh towards Secondary Education with regard to management.

Interpretation: It came to light that the calculated t-value 0.935 is less than the table values 1.96 at 0.05 level and 2.58 at 0.01 level of confidence. Therefore, the null hypothesis is accepted. In the light of this, it can be concluded that there exists no significant difference in the attitude of government and private secondary school students of Arunachal Pradesh towards Secondary Education with respect to management variable. The difference in the mean scores between the two is not significant but the attitude of students in private secondary schools are little higher than the attitude of government secondary school students of Arunachal Pradesh with the mean score difference of 1.07.

Objective IX: To find out the Functions of Secondary Education from the State Government Officials of Arunachal Pradesh.

Findings:

- As per the Secondary Education Policy in Arunachal Pradesh, some of the programmes are not functioning well in the state which include Vocational Education, Science inspired Award MANAV, Girls' incentives, and IEDSS.
- There are various problems relating to teacher posting such as political involvement, minister's interference, medical ground, no proper rule regarding teacher posting, terrain, criss-cross road or topography of the posting place, etc.
- Regarding posting duration, the education officers indicated that there is no rule but some responded that posting duration is 3 years (for RMSA teachers—non-transferable and for state government teachers—as per Commission).
- There was a variation in understanding the teacher-student ratio for secondary schools as some indicated it to be 1:40.

- To a question relating to whether the authority face hindrance/political pressure at the time of teacher recruitment, 66.66% of these officers responded 'Yes' and the remaining 33.33% 'No'. This shows that authority mostly face hindrance and political pressure during teacher recruitment.
- From the officers' responses, it is clear that there are some problems while selecting quality/skilled teachers such as political pressure, corruption, age bar, untrained teachers, language problem, money power, restriction on the selection of non-APST teachers particularly in Science and Mathematics subjects, and so on.
- The state authority takes action against absentee teachers in various ways which includes issuance of show cause notice to the absentee teachers, suspension and termination in case of contractual teachers, hold up of pay and allowance, issuance of warning letter, reduction of salary, and sometimes these teachers are simply scolded by Head of the school.
- To stop backdoor entry during teacher recruitment process, some of the suggestions made by the education officers were recorded. Recruitment responsibility should be shifted to Arunachal Pradesh Public Service Commission (APPSC) and Staff Selection Board (SSB); Mass Media involvement in recruitment process, mass recruitment for whole state to be conducted once in a year, and only candidate who have cleared APTET/ CTET to be allowed.
- For the provision to stop school boundary land encroachment, they have suggested: serving eviction order to be given to illegal encroachers; FIR to be lodged; take help from public and administration team, Gram Panchayat, local people, CO, SMDC, etc.; fund made available to construct boundary wall before establishment of the school; Media, public, elite, youths, and social thinkers, all should come together in common platform to raise voice against this; and

district authority under DC should conduct survey in existing secondary schools to perceive status of school campus and check campus encroachment.

- Regarding defunct schools in Arunachal Pradesh which were observed after the declaration of CBSE results, the officers suggested that Defunct school may be shut down and teachers of these schools to be shifted to schools where teachers are required; degraded to Upper Primary school; proper care and assistance to be given to such schools for up-gradation; up-graded to residential schools with posting of regular Headmaster; and reasons for the defunct to be found out and take important steps for functioning of the particular school.
- Some of the important problems of secondary education were indicated by these officers which include no quality education and irregular classes, insufficient funds, no laboratory and its equipments, many schools are functioning without Headmaster, insufficient teachers and absence of subject teachers especially Mathematics and Science, overcrowded students/student-teacher ratio is not maintained, lack of teacher quarters, electricity, school boundary wall, no internet connectivity, irregularity among teachers as well as students, and no punishment for absenteeism among them.

Functions relating to the development of Secondary Education:

- RMSA programme has been functioning as per the policy guidelines in Arunachal Pradesh according to the responses of 93.33% of the education officers.
- State policy programme such as CMSSY, Vidya Scheme, incentives to girls' education, IEDSS, no retention programme, SSA, RMSA, CCE, ISSE, Samagra Shiksha Abhiyan, CWSN, Shaala Siddhi, and Adhunik Patshala Yojna, etc. are effectively implemented according to Education Officers of the

state but Vocational Educations (IT and TT) are yet to be implemented in the state.

- Most of these officers (66.66%) are not satisfied with the existing infrastructure facilities in the schools of Arunachal Pradesh except for the few (33.33%).
- 73.33% officers explained that buildings and rooms are inadequate. Likewise, 60% explained that furniture is inadequate. According to 66.66% of them, classroom/ blackboard/fans are inadequate. 80% of them revealed that library and sport items are in adequate and 66.66% revealed the inadequacy of laboratories in the schools.
- According to 86.66% of the officers, the state do not have separate grievance redressal cell for the secondary education.
- Based on the responses of 60% of the officers, the funds released to the institutions are not satisfactory.
- The department organizes inspection visits whenever required, once in a month, and yearly, district-wise, and some of them indicated that it is not regular.
- The team committee members of the inspection team in the state are DDSE, Block Education Officer (BEO), BRCC, CRCC, DSE, CO, DC, Local administration officer, and area block functionaries.
- The education department provides scholarship to the students according to 99.33% of the respondents in the study.
- Only 20% of the officers displayed satisfaction over the present performance of secondary schools.
- There is no provision for Vocational Education at the secondary school stage according to the responses of 86.66% of Education Officers.
- The suggestions of the officers for the improvement of the secondary education include posting of required numbers of subject teachers and regular Headmaster in every school, textbooks to be sent in advance and

admission to be done on time, transference in fund, completion of syllabus by all the teachers, teachers to be accommodated in school campus, student-teacher ratio to be maintained, teacher-training should be conducted time to time, political interference should be totally stopped, compulsory entrance exam to be conducted to select students for admission, and regularity of teachers may be recorded and should be encouraged.

Discussion of the Findings

In view of the findings of the study pertaining to the common problems faced by the secondary school students of Arunachal Pradesh, it is to be noted that the most acute problem faced by them is rural-urban imbalance. Especially in Arunachal Pradesh, the schools located in the rural areas are connected to problems such as shortage of subject teachers in Mathematics and Science; having no access to basic infrastructure facilities such as safe drinking water and no separate toilets for boys and girls; limited co-curricular activities; absenteeism among teachers; lack of science laboratory, library, and computers; and absence of vocational course. Generally, both in government and private secondary schools, teachers use traditional methods of teaching. In addition to this, it was found that most of the schools teachers do not complete the syllabus on time.

In such situations and circumstances, it becomes impossible to expect creativity and innovative ideas from the students as well as overall development. Therefore, the educational aim of Gandhiji on 'All round development' fails to meet its goal. Children studying under such conditions would not yield good performance and even though they perform well and achieve good academic performance in the academic years of these schools, there is a possibility that they will be unable to compete with the students of outside world after holding degrees in terms of knowledge and skills. They may also lack confidence for higher education.

It is one of the major findings in the present study that the pass percentages of students in the secondary schools run by the state Government from the past to the present years have shown that Government schools are lacking behind the Private schools in academic performance. From the U-DISE source, it is understood that the average pass percentage of 10th grade students in the government secondary schools during the academic years 2013 to 2017 mostly falls between 50% to 70% whereas, private secondary school students have their average pass percentage mostly falling between 90% to 100%. Therefore, there are many issues to address for the achievement disparity of secondary schools and the students in Arunachal Pradesh. These findings mingle with the earlier findings of *Ghose* (1977), *Medhi* (1978), *Govinda* (1980), *Gogate* (1982), *Marak* (1982), *Mishra* (1983), *Doraiswamy* (1985), *Anwar* (1988), *Bhutto* (1988), *D'Leema* (1988), *Teerapong* (1988), *Jala* and *Langstien* (1989), *Ramana, G.V.* (1989), *Rehman* (1989), *Mittal* (1990), *Panda* (1995), *Mohanti* (2007), *Matthew* (2013), *Singh, T.T.* (2016), *Suham* (2017), and so on. On the other hand, there are some of the positive factors which enhance not only the intellectual growth but overall development of the students. The evidence can be viewed from the secondary education sources of the state as the sources reveals that the secondary school students of private management schools scored much higher than the government secondary school students in terms of academic achievement over the years. Therefore, private secondary schools are great boon to the state of Arunachal Pradesh in terms of secondary education.

In general, the findings also reveal some common problems faced by the teachers in the government secondary schools that despite drawing good salary and having a secured job, the government secondary school teachers serving in various districts of Arunachal Pradesh are dissatisfied with the posting areas particularly in the rural areas due to lack of infrastructure facilities, no facilities for accommodation, decayed infrastructure facilities, unhygienic toilets, no safe drinking water facilities, lack of motivation to teach, not familiar of using ICT or smart classrooms, overburden administration task, and additional periods assigned to them on non-specialized subjects. The findings are also supported by the findings of *Karmayoki* (1974),

Balieh (1882), *Panda* (1985), *Anwar* (1988), *Jala* and *Langstien* (1989), *Roa* (1990), *Deka* (1991), *Khader* (1992), *Nyori* (1992), *Juereemiah Mutuku Kalai* (2006), *Ekundayo, HaastrupTimilehin* (2010), *Smet, Bourgonjon, Wever, Schellens* and *Valcke* (2012), *Ahmad, Rehman, Iqbal, Ali, Budshah* (2013), *Matthew* (2013), *Tarannum* (2016), *Dalchandra* (2018), and so on.

Further, the investigator in the same context found dissatisfaction among the Government Education Officers regarding the poor performance of the secondary students and the existing dilapidated infrastructure facilities in the state of Arunachal Pradesh. As per the responses of the education officers, some of the suggestive remarks were given for the improvement of the secondary education which include posting of required numbers of subject teachers and appointment of regular Headmaster in every school, supply of textbooks in advance and on time admission, transparency, completion of syllabus by all the teachers, accommodation of teachers in school campus, ensuring good pupil-teacher ratio, induction of teacher-training programme for quality education, no involvement of financial power, favouritism, and nepotism during recruitment, local area development fund must be allowed to use for school maintenance, parental involvement, shut down of defunct school, teacher transfer to needy schools, fund for construction of boundary wall in every schools, community support, teacher efficiency and accountability, fair and transparent recruitment, regularity of teachers, no release of salary for absentee teachers, and provision of Career Counselling Cell in every secondary school.

In a nutshell, there is no iota of doubt that secondary education is the corner stone for higher education. The super structure of higher education solely depends upon the quality control, structure, and the administration of secondary education. If secondary education is absent from the quality and adequate facility enhancement leading towards higher education, in this context the educational implications, suggestions, and the overall findings of the present study will be a ray of hope for the future development of the secondary education.

Educational Implications of the Study

The educational implications of the present study indicate practical utility of the findings of the study. It is very important to take note of the implications of the study undertaken in order to reflect and throw light to the significance of the findings. The focus of the present study was on the development and problems of secondary education in Arunachal Pradesh. Therefore, based on the findings of the study, some of the important educational implications are drawn which are discussed below:

1. The finding of the study indicates that there have been an increasing number of schools and teachers in both the Government and Private Secondary schools of Arunachal Pradesh from the academic sessions 2013 to 2017 except for the year 2014, but the practical fact is that there are many unrecorded defunct schools found in some districts and teacher absentees in the interior posting place, such Defunct school may shut down and teachers to be shifted to schools where teachers are required. Therefore, more intense research can be conducted in order to find solution to the problem related to the defunct numbers of schools and the absentee teachers, and the state educational mechanisms should take stringent disciplinary and administrative action against such schools and teachers.
2. In every year from 2013 to 2017, the enrolments of students at 10th grade was more than the enrolment of 10+2 grade students in the government schools of Arunachal Pradesh. This may be because of discontinuation of students in higher studies due to shortage of hostel facility, vocational skill courses, and unattractive physical activities at the secondary level. In this perspective the Government should take initiatives to implement compulsory vocational courses, adequate boarding facility, and physical sports trainers in the schools which may suffice the problem.
3. One of the findings of the study reveals that the private secondary schools are better than the government secondary schools in terms of infrastructure facilities,

especially transportation service, separate toilets, safe drinking water, library, laboratory, etc. It is understood that the infrastructure facility can be an indicator of academic achievement among the students. The present study also explains the status and requirements of infrastructure facilities and about the necessary actions to be taken especially in the government schools by making compulsory regular monitoring and supervision and then to follow up time to time by the state education department without compromising the quality.

4. Apart from the infrastructure facility, academic achievements of the students have improved substantially over the year in the private schools in comparison to the government school. The findings give an indication to the fact that performances of government schools are very poor. Therefore, some innovative steps should be taken to address such problems through the Public Private Partnership to exchange ideas, subject teachers to be accountable in syllabus completion, adopting dynamic methods of teaching, legal actions over private tuition, non-disbursement of salary of absentee teachers, removal of school teachers and corrupt officers, induction on quality teachers training, and appointment of efficient subject teachers particularly sufficient Math and Science teachers. Above all fair and transparent recruitment process will definitely improve the performance of the students and bring quality education in the state.
5. On the basis of the finding of the study, it is revealed that the quality of examination in private secondary schools was better than government secondary schools. It is recommended that government should formulate strict policy on monitoring and evaluating examination system in government secondary schools. Steps should be taken for smooth evaluation of students answer papers by experienced teachers.

6. Findings reveal that majority of the government secondary school teachers are not comfortable to take smart classes due to lack of training and hesitation to adapt new innovative technique. In such cases compulsory technical training should be organized by the schools for proper utilization of the smart classrooms.
7. Findings also reveal that school working hours are not maintained uniformly. At least every school should run up to 2 pm every day so as to retain children in school campus under the intensive care of the teachers and not only to be confined to teaching of five subjects per day. Apart from DDSE/DPO in district level, post of school inspections in district level must be created to timely inspect every school for ensuring proper and smooth functioning of school. Moreover, BEO, BRPs, BRCC, and CRCC must be authorized to inspect the schools twice a week and upload the report with the photographs on District whatsapp.
8. The findings also indicated that the CCE as the evaluation pattern is not favoured by most of the teachers and students of government and private secondary schools of Arunachal Pradesh. As per the opinion of the teachers most of them have opted for the existing external board exam system of evaluation. It is therefore, suggested that the evaluation pattern should be properly studied and examined that would help in bringing out better ways to evaluate students' performance.
9. From the findings it is learnt that the government school teachers prefers Hindi language as a medium to communicate with the students in every subjects but there is a provision to write the exams in English medium only except for Hindi subject and, thus, students are facing problems in translation of the languages in the exam papers and thereby, unable to secure good marks in the examination. It is a major

factor for deterioration of quality education and learning outcomes in the state.

10. The findings reveal that most of the government secondary school teachers had general awareness of the RTE Acts and its intervention but very few of them have undergone such training on RTE Acts. Therefore, from time to time compulsory training should be organized by the state Government.
11. In the findings, it was found that majority of the government secondary schools are not conducting co-curricular activities regularly due to lack of fund, absence of physical trainers, and lack of minimum facilities in the campus. Hence, government is expected to provide sufficient funds to the government secondary schools for bridging the gaps.
12. From the study it is found that government schools have no guidance and counselling cells or vocational courses to address the problems and interest of the students. Therefore, it is suggested to implement compulsory vocational courses and guidance cells in the secondary schools.
13. On the basis of the findings of the study, it is revealed that the quality of education in private secondary schools was better than government secondary schools. Therefore, it is recommended that the government should take steps for quality improvements of education in government secondary schools. Teachers should be instructed to take classes on the basis of annual curricular plan. It is further recommended that school managing committee and PTA should take active role in school developmental activities.
14. The findings indicate that most of the government secondary schools have no proper boundary walls. Therefore, it is suggested that fund should be made available by the government to construct boundary wall before establishment of the school in order to avoid encroachment of school campus.

15. The overall attitude of secondary school students towards the secondary education was high. It also indicated that the secondary school students were positive towards the secondary education. This positive attitude is connected to the satisfaction and expectation of students towards the development of secondary education. Therefore, it is recommended that the secondary education may move forward for its development by implementing all the schemes and programmes in right direction as per the policy framework.

Suggestions for the Further Studies

The investigator completed the present piece of study with every care and after completion of the research project, she has put forward some suggestions for further studies. They are:

1. The present study was confined to the problems of school students and teachers under secondary level. So, the investigator here suggests that such type of study may be conducted in the college and university level too.
2. The investigator suggests studies to be conducted on the study habits among the students of Primary and Higher Secondary Schools in Arunachal Pradesh.
3. The study may be done on comparative bases on the Financial Management in the Government and Private Secondary Schools in the state also.
4. Further, it suggests to study on constructivist approach in the secondary schools of Arunachal Pradesh and various other states in India.
5. The study may be taken up on comparative study on Academic Achievements among the Science and Arts Students.
6. The study may be carried out on the relationship between Head-in-Charge and the Teachers of Higher Secondary Schools in the states in India.

7. The researcher further suggests to study on the assessment of the effectiveness of Teacher-Training Programmes and the role of Teacher Educators in the teacher training colleges.
8. Use of media and ICTs in teaching-learning process in the classrooms by the Secondary and Higher Secondary School Teachers can also be conducted.
9. It also suggests to study the working conditions and professional respect for the Headmasters/Principals and the Teachers of Higher Secondary Schools in Arunachal Pradesh.
10. Comparative study on the Development and Problems of Secondary Education in the states of Manipur and Arunachal Pradesh or between Arunachal Pradesh and other states/UTs of India can also be conducted.
11. An investigation on the effectiveness of trained and untrained Headmasters/Principals and the Teachers at Elementary, Secondary, and Higher Secondary Schools should also be conducted.
12. The study may be taken up on the role of School Management Committee (SMC) and Village Education Committee (VEC) in the development of School Education.

Conclusion

In a nut shell, it can be summed up that education is the pillar to success and when it comes to educational scenario, Secondary Education plays a very significant role. The Secondary Education is the link between Elementary and Higher Secondary Education. It is a crucial stage in the educational ladder as it assists the students in the change of behaviour for future contributions and the world of work. Therefore, it should be reorganized when it is surrounded by several problems and associated to the development. The study undertaken had its major focus on the development and problems of secondary education in Arunachal Pradesh. On the basis of inter analysis of the overall findings it revealed that in terms of growth of secondary schools, numbers of teachers and enrolment of students, the secondary education has been pacing in spectacular wise but in terms of academic achievement of the students, particularly government secondary school students, have been under progressing over the years. In this context, government and also the stakeholders are working together to solve various educational problems regarding lack of infrastructure facility, teacher related problems, administration, management, financial, student's related problems, and so on.

Last but not the least, the move towards solving various educational problems and the thrust for its development should be made the prime focus and a continuous process.

Bibliography

Abidin, M.J.Z., Mohammadi, M.P. & Alzwari, H. (2012). EFL students' attitudes towards learning English language: The case of Libyan secondary school students. *Asian Social Science*. 8 (2), 119.

Aggarwal, J.C. & Guptas (2013). *Secondary Education and Management*. Delhi: Shipra Publication.

Ahmad, Rehman, Iqbal, Ali & Budshah (2013). A study of problems of government secondary school system in Pakistan: Critical analysis of literature and findings a way forward. *International Journal of Academic Research in Business and Social Sciences*. February, Vol. 3, No. 2 ISSN: 2222-6990.

Appalwar, A. & Roa, M. (1995). *Evaluation of Administration of Secondary School of Adilabad and Karimnagar District of Andhra Pradesh with Special reference to Headmasters* (Unpublished Ph.D. thesis). Nagpur University, Maharashtra.

Anwar, J. (1992). *A Comparative study of the Problems experienced by Secondary School Teachers under different Management in Andhra Pradesh and the impact on performance of students* (Unpublished Ph.D thesis). Osmania University, Hyderabad.

Austin, G. & Reynolds, D. (2001). Managing for Improve Schools Effectiveness. *An International Survey Organization*. Vol. 10. No. 2.

Azad, J.L. (2001). 'Financing of Secondary Education'. Paper presented in National Conference: Focus Secondary Education, February 14-16, 2001, NIEPA, New Delhi.

Balieh, T.R. (1984). *A study of the Administration of Secondary Schools in Meghalaya* (Unpublished M.Phil thesis). North Eastern Hill University, Shillong.

Begi, J.U. (2007). *Education in Arunachal Pradesh since 1947 (Constraints, opportunities, initiatives and needs)*. New Delhi: Mittal Publications.

Best, J.W. & Khan, J.V. (2003). *Research in Education*. New Delhi: Prentice Hall of India.

Bhatia, G.H.S. (2018). *Secondary Education*. New Delhi: APH Publishing Corporation.

Bhatnagar, R.P. & Aggarwal, V. (2012). *Educational, Administration, Supervision, Planning And Financing*. Meerut, R. Lall Book Depot.

Bhuyan, C.K. (1969). A page from the education Commissioner's Report: *The* School Complex and NEFA'. *Information*. Vol. III. No. II, Jan.

Biswas, N.B. (1996). Development of Education Arunachal Pradesh. *Arunachal University Research Journal*, Vol. 1 1996.

Biswas, N.B. (1995). Cultural Condition of Learning and Educational Planning in Arunachal Pradesh: Some Thoughts and Issues. *Arunachal Review*, Vol. IV, No. 10.

Biswal, K. (2011). Secondary Education in India: Development Policies, Programmes and Challenges. In: CREATE Pathways to Access Series, Research Monograph Number 63. Page Nos. 1-57.

Buch M.B. (ed). *Third Survey of Research in Education*. (1978-83). New Delhi: NCERT 1987.

Census of India. (2001). Arunachal Pradesh, Provisional Population of 2001, Itanagar.

Chakravorty, B.M. (1991). A study of Repeated Courses among Secondary Students in Ontario. *The Journal of Educational Research*, Vol. XVII, No. 1.

Chudgar, A. & Quin, E. (2012). Relationship between private schooling and achievement: Results from rural and urban

India. *Economics of Education Review*. Vol-31, Issue 4, 376-390.

Dalchandra, M. (2018). *An empirical study of school management for quality education in Southern Rajasthan* (Unpublished PhD thesis). Mohan Lal Sukhadia University, Udaipur.

Das, D. (2007). Scenario of Secondary Education in Chhattisgarh. *Challenges for Secondary Education in India*. National University of Education Planning and Administration, New Delhi.

Dash, J. (1999). *Trends and Problems of Higher Education of Scheduled Tribes in Orissa*. D.Lit. Education, Utkal University. Sixth Survey of Educational Research.

Daver (2005). *Management of Education*. University News. Vol. 43, No. 16.

Diengdoh, L. (2014). *A study on Management and Problems of Secondary Schools in Meghalaya* (Unpublished PhD thesis). North Eastern Hill University: Meghalaya.

Deka, B.N. (1991). *Secondary Education of Assam with reference to Darrang District: An analytical Study* (Unpublished Ph.D. thesis). North Eastern Hill University, Shillong.

Directorate of Economics & Statistics (2010). Statistical abstract of Arunachal Pradesh 2009, Itanagar.

Directorate of School Education (2009). Educational Statistics 2008-09, Itanagar.

Director of School Education (2010). Educational Statistics 2009-10, Itanagar.

Duraiswamy, P. & Subramaniam, T.P. (1999). The Relative Effectiveness of Public and Private Higher Secondary School in an Urban Centre in India. *Journal of Education Planning and Administration*, 13 (1), pg. 37-52.

Ekundayo, Haastrup, & Timilehin (2010). Administering Secondary Schools in Nigeria for Quality Output in the 21st Century: The Principals Challenge. *European Journal of Educational Studies*. 2 (3), ISSN 1946-6331.

Executive Summary Secondary education Research Report (2011). "Status of Secondary Education in Hardoi, Uttar Pradesh and Sambalpur, Orissa.

Fonseca, J. (1996). Secondary School Education in Twenty-First Century. *The Progress of Education*. Vol. LXXI, No. 5.

Garrett, H.E. (2007). *Statistics in Psychology and Education*. New Delhi: International Publisher.

Gay, L.R. & Airasian, P.W. (2000). *Educational Research: Competencies for Analysis and Application*. New Jersey: Prentice-Hall, Inc., pp. 44-45.

Ghose, A. (1977). *A Study of Backwardness in Secondary Schools of West Bengal*. Kalyan University, West Bengal.

50 years Pace of Development in Arunachal Pradesh (1947-1997). Directorate of Economics and Statistics, Government of Arunachal Pradesh, Itanagar.

Government of India, Ministry of Education (1948). *Report of Radhakrishnan Commission*, New Delhi.

Government of India, Ministry of Education, (1952-1953). *Report of the Secondary Education Commission*, 17-25.

Government of India. *Report of the Secondary Education Commission (1952-53)*. Ministry of Education and Social Welfare, 1972.

Government of India. *Report of the Education Commission. 1964-66. Education and National Development*. Ministry of Education, 1978.

Government of India. *National Policy of Education-1986*. New Delhi: (Department of Education) Ministry of Human Resource Development, 1986.

Government of India. *Programme of Action, National Policy on Education-1986*. New Delhi: (Department of Education) Ministry of Human Resource Development, 1986.

Govinda, R. (1983). School Education in Rural Areas. A Study of Tunkur District, ISCC Bangalore. *Third Survey of Educational Research*, New Delhi, NCERT.

Kapoor, K.C. (2003). Process of Education and problems of Tribal's, Learners of Arunachal Pradesh, Rajiv Gandhi University, Rono Hills, Itanagar.

Kapoor, M.M., Vadhera, R.R. & Majumdhar, S. (1994). *Educational Administration in Arunachal Pradesh*. New Delhi: Vikash Publishing House Pvt. Ltd.

Kaul, C.L. & Gupta, J.K. (1992). A Sample Study if School Library Facilities and their Utilization in Secondary and Higher Secondary School of four selected states. *Fifth Survey of Educational Research*. Vol. II. NCERT.

Kaul, L. (1984). *Methodology of Educational Research*. New Delhi: Vikas Publishers.

Khader, M.A. (1992). Analysis of the difference between Private and Public Schools on their Effectiveness on School Achievement. Independent Study, Mysore: Regional College of Education. Mysore. *Fifth Survey of Educational Research*. Vol. II.

Khan, M.Q. & Rikam, N.T. (2000). Rays of Education in Arunachal Pradesh: A Perspective Study. *Arunachal Review*. Vol. IV No. 31.

Kothari, C.R. (2009). *Research Methodology (Methods and Techniques)*. New Delhi, New Age International (P) Ltd.

Majumdar, T.R. (1988). *A Study of Secondary School Education in Calcutta: A Study of the Total System* (Unpublished Ph.D. thesis). Calcutta University, Kolkata.

Mahesha, G. (1992). *A Critical study of some Problems at the + 2 stage of Education in Karnataka* (Unpublished Ph.D. thesis). Karnataka University, Dharwad.

Matthew, Ige. Akindele (2013). Provision of secondary education in Nigeria: Challenges and way forward. *Journal of African Studies and Development* 5.1: n.pag. Web 18th September 2013. http://www.academicjournals.org

Marak, P.R. (1982). *A Survey of School of West Garo Hills District with Special Reference to Physical Infrastructure available in the institution, Position of the Staff; The Enrolment of the Students and High School Leaving*

Certificates (HSCL) Examination Result (Unpublished M.A. Dissertation). North Eastern Hill University, Shillong.

Mbugua, Z.K., Miriti, J.M., Muthaa, G.M. & Riche, G.N. (2012). Challenges Faced by Deputy Head Teacher's in Secondary Schools Administration and Strategies they use to tackle in Imenti South District, Kenya. *International Journal of Educational Planning & Administration.* ISSN: 2249-3093, Vol. 2, November, pp. 45-53, http://www.ripublication.com/ijepa.htm.

Mishra, B.M. (1984). Educational Administration in Orissa. D.Lit. Utkal University. *Fourth Survey of Educational Research* Vol. II.

Mishra, R.K. (1983). *A Critical Study of Administration of Secondary Education in Rural Areas of Faizabad Division* (Unpublished Ph.D. thesis). Avadh University, Faizabad.

Mohapatra, T. (1992). *Problems of Secondary School Teachers: A Comparative Study of Government and Private School Teachers* (Unpublished Ph.D. thesis). Utkal University, Bhubaneswar.

Moorosi, P. (2010). South African female principals' career paths: Understanding the gender gap in secondary school management. *Educational Management Administration and Leadership*. 38 (5), 547-562.

MHRD (2011). Statistics of School Education 2009-2010. MHRD, Government of India. New Delhi: Government of India.

NCERT (1992). Fifth All India Educational Survey (Volume I and II). NCERT, New Delhi.

Ngware, Moses, W., Wamukurri, K. David, & Odebero, S. O. (2006). *Total Quality Management in Secondary Schools in Kenya: Extent of Practice*. Quality Assurance in Education Vol. 14: Issue 4: pp. 339-64.

NIEPA (1993). *A Journal of Educational Planning and Administration Research in India.*

Nyokir, A. *Status of Secondary School Education in Arunachal Pradesh* (Unpublished PhD thesis). Rajiv Gandhi University: Doimukh. 2011.

Nyori, M. *A Study of Educational Administration Set up of Arunachal Pradesh* (Unpublished M.Ed. Dissertation). Arunachal University, Doimukh. 1992.

Pal, S. (2010). Public infrastructure, location of private schools and primary school attainment in an emerging economy. *Economic of Education Review*. 29 (5), 783-94.

Pajankar, Vishal D., and Pajankar, Pranali V. (2013). Development of School Education Status in India. *Department of Educational Survey and Data Processing*, 2010: n.pag New Delhi: NCERT, Web 18th September 2013. www.krepublishers.com

Patel, N.A. (2017). *To study the leadership management of principals and institutional atmosphere of secondary schools* (Unpublished PhD thesis). Saurashtra University, Rajkot.

Pati, S. (1992). *A Study of the Administrative and Supervisory Problems of Secondary School Headmasters of Cuttack-I Circle, Cuttack* (Unpublished M.Phil. thesis). Utkal University, Bhubaneswar.

Purohit, P.N. (2003). *Methodology of Educational Research Tools and Techniques*. Jaipur, India: Mangal Deep Publications.

Rehman, A.M.R. (2002). Missing Tribe of Assam: Some Aspects of their Primary and Secondary education. *Indian Education Review*. Vol. 24 (3).

Rwandema, J. (2017). *A study of academic achievement of secondary school students in relation to their achievement motivation, study habits and learning styles in Kigali city Rwanda* (Unpublished PhD thesis). University of Mysore, Mysore.

Samsuddin (1997). A peep into the Education Commission Report. *Progress of Education* (Poona), XLII, 99-102.

Singh, T.T. (2016). *A Study of the Management Problems of Un-aided Private Secondary Schools of Manipur* (Unpublished Ph.D thesis). Maharaja Sayajirao University, Baroda.

State Prospective Plan on Teacher Education. Department of Education, Government of Arunachal Pradesh, 2002-07.

Suham, J. (2017). *A Study of Management and Problems of Secondary Schools in Tirap District of Arunachal Pradesh* (Unpublished M.ed thesis). Rajiv Gandhi University, Doimukh, Arunachal Pradesh.

Sujatha, K. & Geetha, R.P. (2011). *Management of Secondary Education in India.* Delhi: Shipra Publications.

Sundin, O. & Carlsson, H. (2016). Outsourcing trust to the information infrastructure in schools: Low search engines order knowledge in education practices. *Journal of Documentation.* 72 (6), 990-1007.

Tarannum, S. (2016). *A study of administrative behavior of Heads and work motivation of teachers in relation to their perception of total quality management of secondary schools* (Unpublished PhD thesis). Karnatak University, Karnataka.

Veenman, S. (1984). Perceived problems of beginning teachers. Review of Educational Research. 54 (2), 143-178, 1984.

Wang, M.T., Hill, N.E. & Hofkens, T. (2014). Parental involvement and African American and European American adolescents' academic, behavioral, and emotional development in secondary school. *Child Development.* 85 (6), 2151-2168.

World Bank, October 2009. Promoting secondary education in India. www.Southasia.oneworld.net.

World Bank (2009). Secondary Education in India; Universalising Opportunity. Human Development Unit, South Asia Region. www.worldbank.org. Page no. 15-16

World Bank, September 2013. India an 'under-performer' in secondary education. www.ibe.unesco.org

Appendices

Appendix - I

QUESTIONNAIRE ON THE PROBLEMS OF THE HEAD-IN-CHARGE OF SECONDARY SCHOOLS IN ARUNACHAL PRADESH

Please fill up the following information

1. Name of the Head-in-Charge: ....
2. Sex: Male/Female
3. Community: Tribal/Non-Tribal
4. Educational Qualification: B.A./B.Sc./B.Com, M.A./M.Sc./M.Com, M.Phil., Ph.D
5. Professional Qualification: Trained (B.Ed/D.Eled/DIET) / Untrained
6. School: Govt. /Private
7. District: ....

Signature with seal

General Instructions:

You are requested to go through the following instructions before answering the questions asked in this questionnaire.

1. There are different type of questions in this questionnaire including questions for 'Yes' or 'No', tick (√) the correct option, suggestions to be provided and so on.
2. You can tick one or more options wherever applicable.
3. Please avoid abbreviations and confusing remarks.
4. There is no time limit to complete this questionnaire but you are requested to complete as early as possible.

5. Kindly answer all the questions with utmost sincerity. While we assure you that all the information provided will be kept confidential and used in research work only.

Field Investigator:

Dr. Boa Reena Tok
Professor
Department of Education
Rajiv Gandhi University (A.P.)

SECTION-A: Infrastructure

1. Does your school have its own land? Yes/No
2. Does your school have your own school building? Yes/No
   If yes, what type of school building you have? (Permanent/Rented)
3. What is the structure of your school building? (Assam type/RCC type/Kaccha)
4. Does your school have sufficient playground? Yes/No
5. Does your school have boundary wall? Yes/No
6. Does your school have motor able road connection? Yes/No
7. Are there any hostel facilities in your school for the students? Yes/No
8. Does your school have sufficient furniture? Yes/No
9. What are the physical conditions of your school classroom? Kindly put a tick (√) mark

Desk and Benches		Blackboard/ White		Fans		Electricity		Properly Ventilated	
Sufficient	Insufficient	In Good condition	Not in good	In order	Not in order	available	Not...	Yes	No

10. Do you have the following facilities in your school? Kindly put a tick (√) mark

Auditorium	Teachers' Quarter	Principal's Office	Staffs' Room	EDUSAT/ Internet connection	Computer Room	Smart Classroom	Store Room

11. Does your school provide Laboratory facilities for Science Students?

    If yes, are the following equipments fully equipped? Kindly put a tick (√) mark

    (a) Laboratory room ( ) Apparatus & equipments ( ) (c) Proper furniture's ( )

12. What types of Audio-Visual Aids provided in your school? Kindly put tick (√) mark

    (a) LCD Projectors ( ) (b) Tape recorder ( ) (c) Computer lab ( ) (d) OHP ( )

13. Do you have School Library? Yes/No

    If yes, kindly put a tick (√) mark

    (a) Adequate books ( ) (b) Equipped furniture ( ) (c) Journals ( ) (d) Encyclopedia ( )

14. Do you get adequate safe drinking water supply in your school? Yes/No

15. Is there any provision for separate toilets for boys and girls in your school? Yes/No

16. Does your school provide First-Aid facilities for the students? Yes/No

17. Does your school have ramp/railing facility for the physically challenged? Yes/No

SECTION- B: Teacher

18. How many teachers are there in your school? .... Male No .... Female No ....

19. Are the numbers of teachers sufficient for your school? Yes/No

20. Do you have sufficient number of Science Teachers? Yes/No

21. Are the teachers punctual in the school? Yes/No

    (a) Very punctual ( ) (b) Rarely punctual

    (c) Not punctual at all ( )

22. Do you have skilled manpower in the school? Yes/No
    Please put a tick (√) or cross (x)

Computer Teacher	Music Teacher	Sports Teacher	NCC/Scouts & Guides Teacher	Yoga Teacher

23. Are the teachers committed towards their Profession?
    Please put a tick (√) mark
    (a) All are committed ( ) (b) Some are committed ( )
    (c) Very few are committed ( )
24. Do the teachers use Teaching Learning Materials/Teaching Aids in the classes? Yes/No
    (a) Very often ( ) (b) Rarely use ( ) (c) Never use ( )

SECTION-C: Curriculum, Co curricular, Teaching-Learning & Evaluation

25. Are you satisfied with the existing Curriculum as per NCFSE 2005? Yes/No
26. Is the existing curriculum relevant, productive, contextual & up-to-date? Yes/No
27. Is the syllabus of secondary grade relevant to the present context? Yes/No
28. Do you find any hard spots in the present curriculum? Yes/No
    Please specify if yes..
    ....
29. Do you find difficulties in the implementation of RMSA scheme? Yes/No
    If Yes, Please specify the difficulties ....
    ....
30. Does your school face problem in organizing co-curricular activities? Yes/No
    If Yes, Please specify..
    ....
31. Does your school take the students to the field trips and excursion? Yes/No
32. Are you satisfied with the attendance of students in your school? Yes/No

33. Are you satisfied with the Academic Performance of the students? Yes/No

34. What is the medium of Instruction used mostly by the teachers? Please put a tick (√) mark

    (a) English ( ) (b) Hindi ( ) (c) Mother tongue ( )
    (d) Both the language ( )

35. What is the frequency assessment of students in your school? Please put a tick (√) mark

    (a) Weekly ( ) (b) Monthly ( ) (c) Quarterly ( )
    (d) Half yearly ( ) (e) Annually ( )

36. What are the main examination & Evaluation problems faced by your school?

    a. ....
    b. ....

    Suggest measures for improvement of examination & Evaluation system in the schools.

    a. ....
    b. ....
    c. ....

37. Which system of Evaluation do you feel most appropriate for the teacher's attainment & holistic learning of the students? Please put a tick (√) mark

    (a) CCE System ( ) or (b) Existing external Board exam

SECTION–D: Management, Finance & Supervision

38. Do the school SMC committee members supportive? Yes/No

39. Does your school have institutional planning? Yes/No

40. In a month how many times do you hold a staff meeting? Please put a tick (√) mark

    (a) Once ( ) (b) Twice ( ) (c) Weekly ( )

    (d) Whenever necessary ( )

41. Does your school maintain the following records? Kindly put a tick (√) mark

Teachers' Attendance	Students; Register	Admission Register	CRC Record	Staff Meeting Record	PTA Meeting	Store Log Book

42. What are the main financial sources of your school (during the last five years)?

Fully State govt. Aid	Central Govt. Aid	Donation	School fees	Any other grant

43. Who prepares your school budget? Kindly specify ....
44. How do you prepare your school budget? Please put a tick (√) mark

    (a) Annually ( ) (b) Half yearly ( ) (c) None ( )
45. Are the school accounts audited annually? Yes/No
46. Do you get financial assistance in time? Yes/No
47. Who visits for the school inspection in your school? Please put a tick (√) mark

    (a) CBSE Team ( ) (b) State Govt. Officials ( )

    (c) Third party monitoring ( )
48. How many times does the inspection/monitoring team visits your school annually?

    (a) Frequently ( ) (b) Periodically ( ) (c) Never visit ( )
49. What are the main problems faced with regard to school management? Kindly specify.

    a. ....

    b. ....

    c. ....

    Suggest some measures for the improvement of your school management.

    a. ....

    b. ....

    c. ....

    d. ....

Appendix - II

QUESTIONNAIRE ON THE PROBLEMS 0F SECONDARY SCHOOL TEACHERS IN ARUNACHAL PRADESH

Please fill up the following information:

1. Name of the Teacher: ....
2. Sex: Male/Female
3. Community: Tribal/Non-Tribal
4. Educational Qualification: B.A./B.Sc./B.Com, M.A./M. Sc./M.Com, M.Phil. Ph.D
5. Professional Qualification: Trained (B.Ed/D.Eled/DIET)/ Untrained
6. School: Govt. /Private
7. District: ....

Signature of the teacher

General Instructions:

You are requested to go through the following instructions before answering the questions asked in this questionnaire.

1. There are different types of questions in this questionnaire including questions for 'Yes' or 'No', tick (√) mark the correct option, suggestions to be provided and so on.
2. You can tick one or more options wherever applicable.
3. Please avoid abbreviations and confusing remarks.
4. There is no time limit to complete this questionnaire but you are requested to complete as early as possible.
5. Kindly answer all the questions with utmost sincerity. While we assure you that all the information provided will be kept confidential and used in research work only.

Field Investigator

Dr. Boa Reena Tok
Professor
Department of Education
Rajiv Gandhi University (A.P.)

SECTION-A: Teaching profession

1. Do you feel satisfy with the teaching job at the secondary level? Yes/No

   If No, specify the reason..

   ....

2. Are you committed towards your teaching profession? Please, put a tick (√) mark Yes/No

   (a) Very Committed ( ) (b) Average committed ( )

   (c) Not committed

3. Are you punctual in the school? Please put a tick (√) mark

   (a) Very punctual ( ) (b) Sometimes ( )

   (c) Not punctual at all

4. Do you follow the code of ethics in your profession? Yes/No

5. Are you interested in organizing seminar/conference/research work? Yes/No

6. Are you aware about the RTE Act and its intervention? Yes/No

7. Have you undergone some training for RTE Act? Yes/No

SECTION-B: Infrastructure

8. Do you have sufficient infrastructure in your staff room? Yes/No

   If No, specify what are lacking behind in.......................

   ....

9. Does your school provide Laboratory facilities for Science Students? Yes/No

   If yes, Kindly put a tick (√) mark or if No then tick cross (x) mark

   (a) Laboratory room ( ) (b) apparatus ( )

   (c) science kits ( ) (d) proper furniture

10. Do you face problem to use Audio-Visual Aids/Teaching-aids in your class? Yes/No

    If yes, specify the reason..

    ....

11. Do you face any problem in the School Library? Yes/No
    If yes, kindly mention the problems..............................

    ....
12. Do you get adequate safe drinking water? Yes/No
13. Are there separate toilets facilities for the teachers? Yes/No
14. Do you get transportation facilities? Yes/No

SECTION-C: Academic, Curriculum & Evaluation

15. Are you satisfied with the existing Curriculum as per NCFSE 2005? Yes/No
16. Are the text books relevant, up-to-date and suitable to the need of the student? Yes/No
17. Is the syllabus of secondary grade emphasizing skilled based knowledge? Yes/No
18. Do you manage to complete your syllabi in time? Yes/No
19. Do you find difficulties in the implementation of RMSA scheme? Yes/No
    If Yes, Please specify the difficulties..............................

    ....
20. Are you satisfied with the attendance & performance of the students? Yes/No
21. Do you use Teaching Learning Materials/Teaching Aids in the classes? Yes/No kindly (√)
    (a) Very Often ( ) (b) Rarely ( ) (c) Never ( )
22. Are you familiar to take class through smart class or CAI? Yes/No
23. Which methods of teaching do you used mostly in your classroom? Yes/No
    If yes, please mention. ....

    ....
24. What is the medium of Instruction mostly used by you in the class? Please put a tick (√)
    (a) English ( ) (b) Hindi ( ) (c) Mother-tongue ( )
    (d) Both English & Hindi ( )

25. In case if you are using Hindi & other mother tongue then what is the reason behind? Kindly mention the reason..

....

26. Which system of Evaluation do you feel most appropriate for the teacher's attainment & holistic learning of the students? Please put a tick (√) mark

    (a) CCE System ( ) or

    (b) Existing external Board exam ( )

27. What are the main examination & Evaluation problems faced by the teachers in your school?

    a. ....

    b. ....

    Suggest measures for improvement of examination & Evaluation system in the schools.

    a. ....

    b. ....

SECTION-D: Management & Administration

28. Is your Head-in-Charge cooperative and come regularly to the office? Yes/No
29. Do you get sufficient leave for attending In-Service Training Programme? Yes/No
30. Does your school have a grievances mechanism/anti corporal punishment cell? Yes/No
31. Does your school authority collect extra fee from the students? Yes/No
32. Do you express your opinion freely before your authority? Yes/No
33. Do you face problem in the release of convergence grant from the school? Yes/No
34. Do you efficiently use teaching skills while teaching in the classroom? Yes/No
35. What are the common problems you observe among the students in your school? Tick (√)

    (a) Indiscipline ( ) (b) Addicted to drug abuse ( )

    (c) Internet/mobile addiction ( ) (d) Indecent dress ( )

36. Which area you mostly face problems as a teacher? Kindly put a tick (√) mark

    (a) Poor salary ( ) (b) heavy workload ( ) (c) lack of Quarter ( ) (d) syllabus completion ( ) (e) Dealing with slow learners ( ) (f) over crowded class ( ) (g) lesson plan preparing ( )

37. How many times in a month does your school hold staff meeting? Please put a tick (√) mark

    (a) Frequently ( ) (b) Sometimes ( )

    (c) Never ( )

38. Do you face difficulties in maintaining any of the following records? Please put a tick (√) mark

Admission Register	Cumulative Record Card	PTA Meeting	Store Logbook	Staff Meeting	Science Lab	Time Table

39. In which of the following areas do you find problems in organizing activities in the school?

Workshop/ Seminar/ Conference	Career counseling	Sports events	Field trips/ Excursion	Literary events	Assembly events	NCC/ Scouts & Guides

40. Does the inspection team visit in your school regularly?

    Yes/No

41. Who visits for the school inspection in your school? Kindly tick (√)

    (a) CBSE Team ( ) (b) State Govt. officials ( )

    (c) School management Team

42. How many times does the inspection team visit your school annually? Kindly put a tick(√)

    (a) Frequently ( ) (b) Periodically ( )

    (c) Never ( )

43. Kindly give your opinion regarding the deteriorating quality education in the secondary schools of Arunachal Pradesh. Kindly mark the most acute cause (s) of the problem

    a. Lack of trained teacher? ( )

    b. Poor Infrastructure? ( )

    c. Poor quality teaching? ( )

    d. Irrelevant curriculum ( )

e. Frequent change of education policies? ( )
f. Lack of funds? ( )
g. Lack of science teacher? ( )
h. Lack of incentives? ( )
i. Insufficient teachers? ( )
j. Lacks innovation? ( )
k. Political interference? ( )
l. Poor monitoring? ( )

44. What are the main problems faced by the teacher with regard to school management? Kindly mention the problems.

....

....

....

....

....

Suggest some measures for the improvement of your school management.

....

....

....

....

....

Appendix - III

QUESTIONNAIRE ON THE PROBLEMS OF SECONDARY SCHOOL STUDENTS OF ARUNACHAL PRADESH

Please fill up the following information:

1. Name of the Student: .... Class: ....
2. Sex: Male/Female
3. Community: Tribal/Non-Tribal
4. Pass Percentage of the Previous Examination: ....
5. Settlement: Urban/Rural
6. School: Govt. /Private
7. District: ....

Signature of the student

General Instructions:

You are advised to go through the following instructions before answering the questions asked in this questionnaire.

1. There are different types of questions in this questionnaire including questions for 'Yes' or 'No' and tick (√) the correct option.
2. You can tick one or more options wherever applicable.
3. Please avoid abbreviations and confusing remarks.
4. There is no time limit to complete this questionnaire but you are requested to complete as early as possible.
5. Kindly answer all the questions with utmost sincerity. While we assure you that all the information provided will be kept confidential and used in research work only.

Field Investigator

Dr. Boa Reena Tok
Professor
Department of Education
Rajiv Gandhi University (A.P.)

1. Do you attend the school regularly? Yes/No
2. Are you satisfied with the teaching learning process in your school? Yes/No
3. Do you face any difficulties in understanding the lessons taught by your teachers? Yes/No

   If yes, please specify the reasons.

No subject knowledge	Lack clarity in explanation	Lack legibility in handwriting	Communication/ Language Problem	Not using teaching Aids

4. What are the physical conditions of your school classroom? Kindly, put a tick (√) mark

Desk and Benches		Blackboard/White board		Fans		Electricity		Properly Ventilated	
Sufficient	Insufficient	Good in condition	Bad in condition	In order	Out of order	available	Not	Yes	No

5. Do you have the following facilities in your school? Kindly put a tick (√) or (X) cross mark

Auditorium Hall	Playground	Hostel Facility	Career Counseling Cell	EDUSAT/ Internet connection	Computer Room	Smart Classroom

6. Does your school provide Laboratory facilities for Science Students? Yes/No
7. In which of the subjects do you face difficulty in learning mostly? Kindly put a tick (√) mark.

Math subject	Science subject	Hindi subject	English subject	Social science subject

8. Do you have School Library? Yes/No

   If Yes, kindly tick (√) or if No then put a (x) cross mark from the following facilities

Sufficient books	Adequate furniture	Librarian	Journals & Encyclopedia	Adequate book Shelves	Novels and magazines

9. Are your teachers punctual in the school? Please put a tick (√) mark

   (a) Very punctual ( ) (b) Sometimes ( )

   (c) Not punctual at all ( )

10. Does your school have resource teachers for the following activities? Please put a tick (√) or (x) cross mark if not available

Computer Teacher	Music Teacher	Sport Teacher	NCC/Scouts & Guides Teacher	Yoga Teacher

11. Does your teacher use Teaching Learning Materials/Teaching Aids in the classes? Yes/No

    (a) Very often ( ) (b) Rarely ( ) (c) Never ( )

12. What types of Teaching Aids does your teacher use in your classroom? Kindly tick (√) or (x)

Maps/globes	Charts	Models	Encyclopedia/ books	No teaching Aids

13. Do you get adequate safe drinking water supply? Yes/No
14. Are there separate toilets for boys and girls in your school? Yes/No
15. Do you get Bus transportation facilities? Yes/No
16. Does the school implement 'Swachh Bharat Abhiyan' in your school? Yes/No
17. Do you feel that your school create social discrimination atmosphere? Yes/No
18. Does your school pressurize to play or seat only with the same gender? Yes/No
19. Is the syllabus of secondary grade relevant to the present context? Yes/No
20. Does your teacher complete your syllabi on time? Yes/No
21. Kindly specify and tick (√) the various co-curricular activities organized in your school

Games	Football	Basketball	Volleyball	Table tennis	Badminton	Cricket/ hokey
Intellectual activities	Debate	Seminar	Quiz	Exhibition	Drawing, painting	Extempore speech
Cultural	Drama	Singing	Dancing	Attire show	Instrumental	Mime play

22. What methods do your teacher mostly used in your classroom? Please put a tick (√) mark

Lecture cum Demonstration	Project method	Experimental method/ Inductive & Deductive	Illustration method

23. What is the medium of Instruction mostly used by the teachers in your school? Please tick (√)

    (a) English ( ) (b) Hindi ( ) (c) Mother tongue ( )
    (d) Both English & Hindi ( )

24. Which system of Evaluation do you feel most appropriate for holistic learning of the students? Please put a tick (√) mark

    (a) CCE System ( ) (b) Existing external Board exam ( )

25. What are the main problems faced by you in the school? Kindly specify.

    ....
    ....
    ....
    ....
    ....

    Suggest some measures for the betterment of your school.

    ....
    ....
    ....
    ....
    ....

Appendix - IV

ATTITUDE SCALE FOR SECONDARY STUDENTS TOWARDS SECONDARY EDUCATION

Name of the Student: (Mr./Ms.): .... Class.............

Sex: Male/female: Social category: Tribe/Non-tribe

Name of the School:...

Settlement: Urban/Rural:

District: ....

Direction: Please read the instructions carefully before responding to any of the statements given in this attitude scale.

a. The main purpose of this attitude scale is to seek your opinion relating to the existing system of Secondary Education in Arunachal Pradesh.
b. The attitude scale contains various statements regarding various aspects of Secondary Education in Arunachal Pradesh.
c. The scale consists of 27 statements in all and for each statement, there are five options such as SA, A, U, D, and SD.

   SA – Strongly Agree

   A – Agree

   U – Undecided

   D – Disagree

   SD – Strongly Disagree
d. Read the statement carefully and select the options based on your opinion by putting mark (√) on the selected options out of the five total options provided in each statement.

Principal Investigator

Dr. Boa Reena Tok
Professor
Department of Education
Rajiv Gandhi University (A.P.)

1. Secondary education solely depends upon quality primary education SA A U D SD
2. Teachers are sincere and regular in their teaching learning activities at the secondary stage. SA A U D SD
3. Secondary education ensures proper mental development of the learners. SA A U D SD
4. Value education is emphasized at the secondary school stage. SA A U D SD
5. Students receive quality education at secondary school stage. SA A U D SD
6. Secondary education makes the learners well aware of the environmental problems. SA A U D SD
7. Our parents do support and encourages us in our studies. SA A U D SD
8. School life creates a holistic development in our personality. SA A U D SD
9. Secondary education may be considered as a foundation stage to inculcate the sense of good citizenship among the learners. SA A U D SD
10. Secondary education inculcates the sense of dignity of labor among the learners. SA A U D SD
11. Secondary education does not provides the base for scientific studies and activities. SA A U D SD
12. The curriculum of secondary school stage are relevant to the needs of the learner. SA A U D SD
13. There is active community participation at the secondary schools. SA A U D SD
14. Village Education Committee extends sufficient cooperation in managing and running the secondary schools. SA A U D SD

15. The regular management in our school time table is rigid. SA A U D SD
16. The monitoring team inspects our school periodically. SA A U D SD
17. Learners imbibe some health habits at the secondary school stage. SA A U D SD
18. There is no scope for Vocational education in the secondary level. SA A U D SD
19. There is least importance given for creative thinking ability. SA A U D SD
20. There is a regular PTA meeting in the school. SA A U D SD
21. The removal of the CCE pattern of evaluation in beneficial for the secondary school students. SA A U D SD
22. Grading system is better than the marking system for the context of secondary education. SA A U D SD
23. CCE was a failure because it could not evaluate students' real learning. SA A U D SD
24. Examination & evaluation are transparent & unbiased in school SA A U D SD
25. Implementation of RMSA scheme brought a change in school. SA A U D SD
26. Secondary school need a separate institutional plan for its progress. SA A U D SD
27. Secondary education in Arunachal Pradesh is preparing the learners for future employment. SA A U D SD

Appendix - V

Interview Schedule for the Government Educational Officers

Profile:

Name of the Officer (Mr./Ms./Dr./Prof.): .... xyz...............

Designation: .... District ....

Office Address: ....

Contact No.: (1) Office: .... (2) Mobile: ....

1. In your opinion does the RMSA programme functioning as per the policy guidelines in our state? Recorded response

   ....

   ....

2. Can you share some of the state policy programmes which are effectively implemented for the quality enhancement in the Secondary Education? Recorded response:

   (i) ....

   (ii) ....

   (iii) ....

3. In your opinion which are the programmes not functioning well as per the Secondary Education policy in the state of Arunachal Pradesh? Recorded response:

   (i) ....

   (ii) ....

   (iii) ....

4. Are you satisfied with the existing infrastructure facilities in the School of A.P? Yes/No

5. Can you tell something about the status and feasibility of infrastructure facilities provided to the schools by the state government?

Whether School facilities are		Adequate?	Inadequate?
1.	Infrastructure (Building/Rooms etc.)		
2.	Furnitures (Table, Chairs, Desks etc.)		
3.	Classroom Blackboard/whiteboard/ fans etc.		
4.	Laboratory Room (Chemicals)		

5.	Library hall with books		
6.	Sports items		
7.	Computer teacher		

6. Do you have a separate grievance redrehssal cell for the Secondary Education in the state of Arunachal Pradesh?

Yes/No

If yes, how does the cell functions? Recorded response:

(i) ....

(ii) ....

7. Please share some of your views in relation to the release of funds to the institution in our state? Is it satisfactory? Does the fund utilized properly? Recorded response:

(i) ....

(ii) ....

8. How often does your departments organize inspection visits to the secondary schools of Arunachal Pradesh? Who are the team committee members?

Recorder response: ....

....

9. Does your department provide scholarship to the students? Yes/No

(a) Merit scholarship (b) ST/SC scholarship

(c) Any other

10. what are the problems regarding teacher posting? Are there any rules for posting duration? What are the ratios for each secondary school?

Recorder response: ....

....

....

11. In your opinion does the authority face hindrance/political pressure at the time of teacher recruitment?

Yes/No

12. Where does the problem lie while selecting quality skilled teachers in A.P?

Recorder response: ....

....

....

13. What are the actions been taken for the absentee teachers by our state Authority?

    Recorder response: ....

    ....

    ....

14. As per your view, can you suggest what steps should be taken to stop the backdoor entry for the teacher recruitment in our state?

    Recorder response: ....

    ....

    ....

15. Is there provision to stop the school boundary land encroachment? Yes/No

    If yes, then kindly share your points...................

16. Are you satisfied with the present performance/result of the secondary schools in A.P? Recorded response If No:

    ....

    ....

    ....

17. There are some defunct schools in A.P which has been observed after the declaration of CBSE results. How will you take up this matter? Please say something.

    Recorder response: ....

    ....

    ....

18. Does the state government keep records of Private schools of A.P? Yes/No

19. Is there any provision for vocational education in secondary schools of A.P?

    Recorder response: ....

    ....

    ....

Recorder response: ....

....

....

20. There are some problems in secondary education as you are aware, can you share something about the existing reality problems which you need to address immediately? Recorded response:

Recorder response: ....

....

....

21. Can you bring an order and effective secondary education in A.P? If yes, how would you like to recommend for the improvement of the present system. Please share something.

Recorder response: ....

....

....

Photographs of Govt. Secondary School Conditions in the State of Arunachal Pradesh

Govt Hr Secondary School Anini

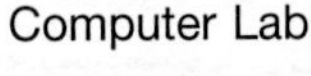

Computer Lab

Govt School Students in Traditional

Students in the Assembly Ground Uniforms

Kacha approach School Road

Dilapidated Govt. School Gate

Congested compound of Govt. School

Classroom without Electricity Connection

Science Laboratory without equipments and outdated Materials

Classroom blackboard Condition

Classroom Infrastructure

Classroom Ceiling in Dilapidated Condition

Classroom Tin Wall Partition

Unrepaired Drinking Water Taps

Unhygienic Drinking Water Provision

Headmaster's Office Condition

Teachers Common Room

Temporary School Boundary Wall

Classroom Extension Structure

Girls Hostel without Boundary Wall

Abandoned Boys Hostel

School Toilets without Water Connection

Dilapidated Teachers Govt. Quarter

Source: Pictures taken during field survey

Index